# Radical
# Forgiveness

# Radical Forgiveness

*A Revolutionary Five-Stage Process to*
- *Heal Relationships*
- *Let Go of Anger and Blame*
- *Find Peace in Any Situation*

## COLIN TIPPING

SOUNDS TRUE

BOULDER, COLORADO

Sounds True, Inc.
Boulder, CO 80306

Cover and book design by Rachael Murray

Printed in Canada


Library of Congress Cataloging-in-Publication Data
Tipping, Colin C.
Radical forgiveness : a revolutionary five-stage process to : heal relationships, let
    go of anger and blame, find peace in any situation / Colin Tipping.
    p. cm.
  ISBN 978-1-59179-764-7 (pbk.)
  1. Forgiveness. 2. Interpersonal relations. I. Title.
  BF637.F67T56 2010
  158.2–dc22
                                      2009029752


10 9 8 7 6 5 4 3 2 1

Dedicated to the memory of
*Diana, Princess of Wales*
who, through her demonstration of the transforming
power of love, opened the heart chakra of
Great Britain and much of the world.

# Contents

# Illustrations & Tables

# Acknowledgments

My gratitude and love goes first to my wife, JoAnn, for believing in me and giving me total support for writing this book, even when times got hard. I also owe a special debt of gratitude to my sister, Jill, and brother-in-law, Jeff, for allowing me to publish a very personal story about them both, without which this book would have been very much impoverished. I also acknowledge Jeff's daughter Lorraine and my daughter Lorraine for the same reason, and all the members of Jill and Jeff's family who were willing to read the book and to see the best in each person who had a part to play in Jill's story. I also acknowledge my brother, John, who witnessed the unfolding of the story, for his patience and support. I owe a special debt of gratitude to Michael Ryce for his inspiration and collaboration on the early version of the forgiveness worksheet, and to Arnold Patent for introducing me to spiritual law. There are countless numbers who have contributed in

ACKNOWLEDGMENTS

very important ways to this book and to the work of spreading the message of Radical Forgiveness and I give thanks daily for every one of them. Thanks are due to all my graduates of the Institute of Radical Forgiveness who are living it and doing it by example and as teachers. Special thanks to Debi Lee for letting me tell her story around the world and to Karen Taylor-Good whose songs and singing add an indescribably wonderful tone to every workshop I do—especially when she's there in person. Special appreciation is due to my co-workers and colleagues at the Institute for Radical Forgiveness Therapy and Coaching, Inc. Finally, my love and gratitude to my mother and my father for choosing to have me and for accepting my request to incarnate through them.

xii

# Introduction

EVERYWHERE WE LOOK—in the newspapers, on TV, and even in our own personal lives—we see examples of people who have been egregiously victimized. We read, for example, that at least one in every five adults in America today was either physically or sexually abused as a child. TV news confirms that rape and murder are commonplace in our communities and crime against people and property is rampant everywhere. Around the world we see torture, repression, incarceration, genocide, and open warfare occurring on a vast scale.

In the early 1990s I began offering forgiveness workshops, cancer retreats, and corporate seminars. Since then I have heard enough horror stories from quite ordinary people to convince me that there is not a human being on the planet who has not been seriously victimized at least once, and in minor ways more times than they could count. Who among us can say they have never blamed someone else for their lack of happiness? For most if not all of us, blame is simply a way of life.

Indeed, the victim archetype is deeply ingrained in all of us, and it exerts great power in the mass consciousness. For eons we have played out victimhood in every aspect of our lives, convincing ourselves that victim consciousness is absolutely fundamental to the human condition. The time has come to ask ourselves this question: how can we stop creating our lives this way and let go of the victim archetype as the model for how to live?

To break free from such a powerful archetype, we must replace it with something radically different—something so compelling and spiritually liberating that it magnetizes us away from victimhood. We need something that will take us beyond the drama of our lives so we can see the big picture and the truth that, right now, lies hidden from us. When we awaken to that truth, we will understand the meaning of our suffering and be able to transform it immediately.

As we continue to move into the new millennium and prepare for the imminent next great leap in our spiritual evolution, it is essential that we adopt a way of living based not on fear, control, and abuse of power but on true forgiveness, unconditional love, and peace. That's what I mean by something radical, and that is what my book is all about: helping us make that transition.

If we are to transform anything, we must be able to experience it completely and fully, which means that to transform the victim archetype, we must first experience victimhood fully. There is no shortcut! Therefore, we need situations in our lives that allow us to feel victimized so we can transform the energy through Radical Forgiveness.

To transform an energy pattern so fundamental as the victim archetype, many, many people—souls who possess the wisdom and love necessary to accomplish this immense task—must awaken and accept this as their spiritual mission. Perhaps you are one of the souls who volunteered for this mission. Could that be why this book speaks to you?

Jesus gave a powerful demonstration of what transforming the victim archetype means, and I believe he now waits patiently and lovingly for us to follow his lead. Up to now, at least, we have failed to learn from his example precisely because the victim archetype has had such a strong hold on our psyches.

We have ignored the lesson of genuine forgiveness that Jesus taught—that there are no victims. We straddle the fence and attempt to forgive while staying firmly committed to being victims. We have made Jesus himself the ultimate victim, and this will not move us forward in our spiritual evolution. True forgiveness must include completely letting go of victim consciousness.

Indeed, my main intention in writing this book was to make clear the distinction between forgiveness that maintains the victim archetype and Radical Forgiveness that frees us from it. Radical Forgiveness challenges us to fundamentally shift our perception of the world and our interpretation of what happens to us so we can stop being victims. My one goal is to help you make that shift.

I recognize that the ideas I am presenting here may be extremely challenging for someone who has been severely victimized and is still carrying a lot of pain. I ask only that you read this book with an open mind and see whether or not you feel better after reading it.

As I write this edition of the book, I can tell you that the feedback I have received from my readers and those who come to my workshops has been overwhelmingly positive. Even people who have been in emotional pain for a long time have found the book to be extremely freeing and healing—and the workshops transformational.

What has also been amazing and gratifying is the extent to which Chapter 1, "Jill's Story," has created immediate healing for many, many people. I originally thought I was writing it as a useful lead-in to the concepts and ideas behind this book, but I now recognize that Spirit knew better and was guiding my hand all the way. I get many phone calls from people—often still in tears—who, having just read the story, tell me that they see themselves in it and feel that their healing has already begun.

A great many of those who call have been moved to share their experience with others by emailing "Jill's Story" directly from my website (see Further Resources at the end of the book) to all their friends, relations, and business associates—a wonderful chain reaction! I shall be forever grateful to my sister and brother-in-law for allowing me to tell their story and making that gift to the world.

I find myself very humbled by the overall response I am getting to the book, and it is fast becoming clear to me that I am being used by Spirit to get this message out so that we can all heal, raise our vibration, and go home. I am grateful to be of service.

*Namasté*
Colin Tipping

*part one*

---

# A Radical Healing

# 1 Jill's Story

*Author's Note: To give you, the reader, an understanding of what I call Radical Forgiveness, I have presented the following true account of how this process saved my sister's marriage and changed her life. Since that time, Radical Forgiveness has positively impacted the lives of countless others, for not long after this episode with my sister, I realized that the process could be used as a form of help quite different from traditional psychotherapy and relationship counseling.* — C.T.

As soon as I saw my sister, Jill, emerge into the lobby of Atlanta's Hartsfield International Airport, I knew something was wrong. She had never hidden her feelings well, and it was apparent to me that she was in emotional pain.

Jill had flown from England to the United States with my brother, John, whom I had not seen for sixteen years. He had emigrated from England to Australia in 1972 and I to America in 1984—thus Jill was, and still is, the only one of the three siblings living in England. John had made a trip home, and this trip to Atlanta represented the last leg of his return journey. Jill accompanied him to Atlanta so she could visit me and my wife, JoAnn, for a couple of weeks and see him off to Australia from there.

After the initial hugging and kissing and a certain amount of awkwardness, we set out for the hotel. I had arranged rooms for one night so JoAnn and I could show them Atlanta the next day before driving north to our home.

As soon as the first opportunity for serious discussion presented itself, Jill said, "Colin, things are not good at home. Jeff and I might be splitting up."

Despite the fact that I had noticed something wrong with my sister, this announcement surprised me. I had always thought she and Jeff were happy in their six-year marriage. Both had been married before, but this relationship had seemed strong. Jeff had three kids with his previous wife, while Jill had four. Her youngest son, Paul, was the only one still living at home.

"What's going on?" I asked.

"Well, it's all quite bizarre, and I don't quite know where to begin," she replied. "Jeff is acting really strange, and I can't stand much more of it. We've gotten to the point where we can't talk to each other anymore. It's killing me. He has totally turned away from me and says that it's all my fault."

"Tell me about it," I said, glancing at John, who responded by rolling his eyes. He'd stayed at their house for a week prior to flying to Atlanta, and I guessed by his demeanor that he'd heard enough of this subject to last him a while.

"Do you remember Jeff's eldest daughter, Lorraine?" Jill asked. I nodded. "Well, her husband got killed in a car crash about a year ago. Ever since then, she and Jeff have developed this really weird relationship. Any time she calls, he fawns over her, calling her 'Love' and spending hours talking to her in hushed tones. You'd think they were lovers, not father and daughter. If he's in the middle of something and she calls, he drops everything to talk with her. If she comes to our home, he acts just the same—if not worse. They huddle together in this deep and hushed conversation that excludes everyone else, especially me. I can hardly stand it. I feel like she has become the center of his life, and I hardly figure in it at all. I feel totally shut out and ignored."

She went on and on, offering more details of the strange family dynamic that had developed. JoAnn and I listened attentively. We wondered aloud about the cause of Jeff's behavior and were generally sympathetic. We made suggestions as to how she might talk to him about his behavior and generally struggled to find a way to fix things, as would any concerned brother and sister-in-law. John was supportive and offered his perspective on the situation as well.

What seemed strange and suspicious to me was the uncharacteristic nature of Jeff's behavior. The Jeff I knew was affectionate with his daughters and certainly codependent enough to badly need their approval and love, but I had never seen him behave in the manner Jill described. I had always known him as caring and affectionate toward Jill. In fact, I found it hard to believe that he would treat her quite so cruelly. It was easy to understand why this situation made Jill unhappy and how Jeff's insistence that she was imagining it all, and making herself mentally ill over it, made it all so much worse for her.

The conversation continued all the next day. I began to get a picture of what might be going on between Jill and Jeff from a Radical Forgiveness standpoint but decided not to mention it—at least not right away. She was too caught up in the drama of the situation and wouldn't have been able to hear and understand what I had to say. Radical Forgiveness is based on a very broad spiritual perspective that was not our shared reality when we were all still living in England. Feeling certain that both she and John were unaware of my beliefs underlying Radical Forgiveness, I felt that the time had not yet arrived to introduce so challenging a thought as "this is perfect just the way it is—and an opportunity to heal."

After the second day of verbally going round and round the problem, I decided the time was near for me to try the Radical Forgiveness approach. This would require that my sister open up to the possibility that something beyond the obvious was happening—something that was purposeful, divinely guided, and intended for her highest good. Yet she was so committed to being the victim in the situation, that I wasn't sure I could get her to hear an interpretation of Jeff's behavior that would take her out of that role. Still, just as my sister began yet another repetition of what she had said the day before, I decided to intervene. Tentatively, I said, "Jill, are you willing to look at this situation differently? Would you be open to me giving you a quite different interpretation of what is happening?"

She looked at me quizzically, as if she were wondering, How can there possibly be another interpretation? It is how it is! I had a certain track record with Jill, though, because I had helped her solve a relationship problem before, so she trusted me enough to say, "Well, I guess so. What do you have in mind?"

This was the opening I was waiting for. "What I'm going to say may sound strange, but try not to question it until I've finished. Just stay open to the possibility that what I'm saying is true, and see whether or not what I say makes sense to you in any way at all."

Until this time, John had done his best to stay attentive to Jill, but the constant repetitive conversation about Jeff had begun to bore him tremendously. In fact, he had largely tuned her out. Now I was acutely aware that my interjection had caused John to perk up and begin listening again.

"What you have described to us, Jill, certainly represents the truth as you see it," I began. "I have not the slightest doubt in my mind that this is occurring just as you say it is. Besides, John has witnessed much of the situation over the last three weeks and confirms your story—right, John?" I queried, turning toward my brother.

"Absolutely," he said. "I saw it going on a lot, just as Jill says. I thought it was pretty strange and, quite honestly, much of the time I felt awkward being there."

"I'm not surprised," I said. "Anyway, Jill, I want you to know that nothing I am going to say negates what you have said or invalidates your story. I believe that it happened the way you said it happened. Let me, however, give you a hint of what might be going on underneath this situation."

"What do you mean, underneath the situation?" Jill asked, eyeing me suspiciously.

"It's perfectly natural to think that everything 'out there' is all there is to reality," I explained. "But maybe there's a whole lot more happening beneath that reality. We don't perceive anything else going on because our five senses are inadequate to the task. But that doesn't mean it isn't occurring.

"Take your situation. You and Jeff have this drama going on. That much is clear. What if, beneath the drama, something of a more spiritual nature was happening—same people and same events, but a totally different meaning? What if your two souls were doing the same dance but to a wholly different tune? What if the dance was about you healing? What if you could see this as an opportunity to heal and grow? That would be a very different interpretation, would it not?"

Both she and John looked at me as if I were now speaking a foreign language. I decided to back off from the explanation and go directly for the experience.

"Looking back over the last three months or so, Jill," I went on, "what did you mostly feel when you saw Jeff behaving so lovingly toward his daughter Lorraine?"

"Anger mostly," she said, but continued thinking about it. "Frustration," she added. Then, after a long pause, "And sadness. I really feel sad." Tears welled up in her eyes. "I feel so alone and unloved," she said and began sobbing quietly. "It wouldn't be so bad if I thought he couldn't show love, but he can and he does—with *her!*"

She spat the last few words out with vehemence and rage and began to sob uncontrollably for the first time since her arrival. She'd shed a few tears prior to this, but she hadn't really let herself cry. Now, at last, she was letting go. I was pleased that Jill had been able to get in touch with her emotions that quickly.

A full ten minutes went by before her crying subsided and I felt she could talk. At that point I asked, "Jill, can you ever remember feeling this same way when you were a little girl?" Without the slightest hesitation, she said, "Yes." She was not immediately forthcoming about when, so I asked her to explain. It took her a while to respond.

"Dad wouldn't love me either!" she finally blurted out, and she began to sob again. "I wanted him to love me, but he wouldn't. I thought he couldn't love anyone! Then your daughter came along, Colin. He loved her, all right. So why couldn't he love me, god-dammit?" She banged her fist hard on the table as she shouted the words and dissolved into more uncontrollable tears.

Jill's reference was to my eldest daughter, Lorraine. Coincidentally, or rather, synchronistically, she and Jeff's eldest daughter have the same name.

Crying felt really good to Jill. Her tears served as a powerful release and possibly a turning point for her. A real breakthrough might not be far away, I thought. I needed to keep nudging her forward.

"Tell me about the incident with my daughter Lorraine, and Dad," I said.

"Well," Jill said, while composing herself. "I always felt unloved by Dad and really craved his love. He didn't hold my hand or sit me on his lap much. I always felt there must be something wrong with me. When I was older, Mum told me she didn't think Dad was capable of loving anyone, not even her. At that time I had more or less made peace with that. I rationalized that if he wasn't really capable of loving anyone, it wasn't my fault that he didn't love me. He really didn't love anyone. He hardly ever made a fuss about my kids—his own grandchildren—much less people or kids not his own. He was not a bad father. He just couldn't love. I felt sorry for him."

She cried some more, taking her time now. I knew what she meant about our father. He was a kind and gentle man but very quiet and withdrawn. For the most part, he certainly had seemed emotionally unavailable to anyone.

As Jill became more composed once again, she continued, "I remember a particular day at your house. Lorraine was probably about four or five years old. Mum and Dad were visiting from Leicester, and we all came to your house. I saw your Lorraine take Dad's hand. She said, "Come on, Granddad. Let me show you the garden and all my flowers." He was like putty in her hands. She led him everywhere and talked and talked and talked, showing him all the flowers. She enchanted him. I watched them through the window the whole time. When they came back in, he put her on his lap and was as playful and joyful as I had ever seen him.

"I was devastated. So he is able to love after all, I thought. If he can love Lorraine, then why not me?" The last few words came out as a whisper followed by deep tears of grief and sadness, tears held in for all those years.

I figured we had done enough for the time being and suggested we make tea. (Well, we're English! We always make tea, no matter what.)

Interpreting Jill's story from a Radical Forgiveness standpoint, I easily saw that Jeff's outwardly strange behavior was unconsciously designed to support Jill in healing her unresolved relationship with her father. If she could see this and recognize the perfection in Jeff's behavior, she could heal her pain and Jeff's behavior would almost certainly stop. However, I wasn't sure how to explain this to Jill in a way she could understand at that point in time. Luckily, I didn't have to try. She stumbled on the obvious connection by herself.

Later that day she asked me, "Colin, don't you think it's odd that Jeff's daughter and your daughter both have the same name? Come to think of it, both of them are blonde and firstborn. Isn't that a strange coincidence! Do you think there's a connection?"

I laughed and replied, "Absolutely. It's the key to understanding this whole situation."

She looked at me long and hard. "What do you mean?"

"Work it out for yourself," I replied. "What other similarities do you see between that situation with Dad and my Lorraine and your current situation?"

"Well, let's see. Both girls have the same name. Both of them were getting what I don't seem to be able to get from the men in my life."

"And what is that?" I inquired.

"Love," she said in a whisper.

"Go on," I urged gently.

"It seems that your Lorraine was able to get the love from Dad that I couldn't. And Jeff's daughter Lorraine gets all the love she wants from her dad, but at my expense. Oh, my God!" she exclaimed. She really was beginning to understand now.

"But why?" she asked in a panic. "I don't understand why. It's a bit frightening! What the heck's going on?"

It was time to put the pieces together for her. "Look, Jill," I said. "Let me explain how this works. This happens to be a perfect example of what I was talking about earlier when I said that beneath the drama we call life lies a whole different reality. Believe me, there's nothing to be frightened about. When you see how this works, you will feel more trust, more security, and more peace than you ever thought possible. You'll realize how well we are being supported by the Universe or God, whatever you want to call it, every moment of every day no matter how bad any given situation seems at the time." I tried to be as reassuring as I could.

"Looked at from a spiritual standpoint, our discomfort in any given situation provides a signal that we are out of alignment with spiritual law and are being given an opportunity to heal something. It may be some original pain or perhaps a toxic belief that stops us from becoming our true selves. We don't often see it from this perspective, however. Rather, we judge the situation and blame others for what is happening, which prevents us from seeing the message or understanding the lesson. This prevents us from healing. If we don't heal whatever needs to be healed, we must create more discomfort until we are literally forced to ask, 'What is going on here?' Sometimes the message has to become very loud, or the pain extremely intense, before we pay attention. A life-threatening illness, for example, provides a loud message. Yet, even when facing death, some people don't get the connection between what is happening in their lives and the opportunity for healing that it provides.

"In your case, what has come up to be healed this time is your original pain around your father and the fact that he never showed you love. That is what all your current pain and discomfort are about. This particular pain has arisen many times before in different situations, but, because you didn't recognize the opportunity before, it never got healed. That's why having yet another opportunity to look at and heal this issue is a gift!"

"A gift?" Jill questioned. "You mean it's a gift because there's a message in it for me? One that I might have gotten a long time ago if I'd been able to see it?"

"Yes. Had you seen it then, you would have had less discomfort and you wouldn't be going through this now.

But no matter—now is fine too. This is perfect, and now you won't have to produce a life-threatening illness to understand this, like so many people do. You're getting it now—you're beginning to understand and to heal.

"Let me explain to you exactly what happened and how it has affected your life up until now," I said, wanting her to understand clearly the dynamics of her current situation.

"As a little girl, you felt abandoned and unloved by Dad. For a girl, this is devastating. From a developmental standpoint, it is necessary for a young girl to feel loved by her father. Since you didn't feel that love, you concluded that there must something wrong with you. You began to really believe you were unlovable and inherently 'not enough.' That belief anchored itself deeply in your subconscious mind and, later, when it came to relationships, began to run your life. In other words, as a way of mirroring your subconscious belief that you were not enough, your life has always included actual situations that exhibit to you the fact that you were, indeed, not enough. Life will always prove your beliefs right.

"When you were a child, the pain of not getting Dad's love was more than you could bear, so you suppressed some of it and repressed a whole lot more. When you suppress emotion, you know it's there, but you stuff it down. Repressed emotion, on the other hand, gets buried so deeply in the subconscious mind that you lose awareness of it.

"Later, when you began to realize that your father was not a naturally loving man and probably couldn't love anyone, you began to somewhat rehabilitate or heal yourself from the effects of feeling unloved by him. You probably released some of the suppressed pain and maybe began to give up some part of the belief that you were unlovable. After all, if he couldn't love anyone, maybe it wasn't your fault that he didn't love you.

"Then along came the bombshell that knocked you right back to square one. When you observed him loving my Lorraine, that triggered your original belief. You said to yourself, 'My father can love after all, but he doesn't love me. It is obviously my fault. I am not enough for my father, and I will never be enough for any man.' From that point on, you continually created situations in your life to support your belief that you are not enough."

"How have I done that?" Jill interrupted. "I don't see how I have created myself not being enough in my life."

"How was your relationship with Henry?" She had been married to Henry, her first husband and the father of her four children, for fifteen years.

"Not bad in many respects, but he was such a woman-izer. Always looking for opportunities to make out with other women. I hated that."

"Exactly. And you saw him as the villain and you as the victim in that situation. But the truth is, you attracted him into your life precisely because, at some level, you knew he would prove your belief about not being enough. By being unfaithful, he would support you in being right about yourself."

"Are you trying to say he was doing me a favor? I sure as heck don't buy that!" she said, laughing, but also with some not-too-well-disguised anger.

"Well, he certainly supported your belief, didn't he?" I replied. "You were so 'not enough' that he always was on the lookout for other women, for 'something more.' If he had done the opposite and consistently treated you as if you were totally enough by being faithful, you would have created some other drama in your life to prove your belief. Your belief about yourself, albeit a totally false one, made it impossible for you to be enough.

"By the same token, had you at that time healed your original pain around your father and changed your belief to 'I am enough,'" Henry would have immediately stopped propositioning your friends. If he hadn't, you would have felt perfectly happy to leave him and find someone else who would treat you as though you were enough. We always create our reality according to our beliefs. If you want to know what your beliefs are, look at what you have in your life. Life always reflects our beliefs."

Jill seemed a bit perplexed, so I decided to reiterate some of the points I had made. "Each time Henry cheated on you, he gave you the opportunity to heal your original pain around being unloved by Dad. He demonstrated and acted out for you your belief that you were never going to be enough for any man. The first few times it happened, you may have gotten so mad and upset that you could have gotten in touch with the original pain and become acquainted with your belief system about yourself. In fact, his first acts of unfaithfulness represented your first opportunities to practice Radical Forgiveness and to heal your original pain, but you missed them. You made him wrong each time and created yourself as a victim instead, which made healing impossible."

"What do you mean, forgiveness?" Jill asked, still looking troubled. "Are you saying I should have forgiven him for seducing my best friend and anyone else he could find who was willing?"

"I am saying that, at that time, he provided you with an opportunity to get in touch with your original pain and to see how a certain belief about yourself was running your life. In so doing, he gave you the opportunity to understand and change your belief, thus healing

19

your original pain. That's what I mean by forgiveness. Can you see why he deserves your forgiveness, Jill?"

"Yes, I think so," she said. "He was reflecting my belief—the one I had formed because I felt so unloved by Dad. He was making me right about not being enough. Is that correct?"

"Yes, and to the extent that he provided you with that opportunity, he deserves credit—actually, more than you realize right now. We have no way of knowing whether he would have stopped his behavior had you healed your issue around Dad at that time—or whether you would have left him. Either way, he would have served you powerfully well. So in that sense, he deserves not only your forgiveness but your deep gratitude as well. And you know what? It wasn't his fault that you didn't understand the true message behind his behavior.

"I know it was hard for you to see that he was trying to give you a great gift. That's not how we are taught to think. We're not taught to look at what is going on and say, 'Look what I have created in my life. Isn't that interesting?' Instead, we are taught to judge, lay blame, accuse, play victim, and seek revenge. Neither are we taught to think that our lives are directed by forces other than our own conscious mind—but, in truth, they are.

"In fact, it was Henry's *soul* that tried to help you heal. On the surface, he just acted out his sexual addiction, but his soul—working with your soul— chose to use the addiction for your spiritual growth. Recognizing this fact is what Radical Forgiveness is all about. Its purpose lies in seeing the truth behind the apparent circumstances of a situation and recognizing the love that always exists there."

I felt that talking about her current situation would help Jill fully understand the principles I had described, so I said, "Let's take another look at Jeff and see how these principles are operating in your current relationship. In the beginning, Jeff was extremely loving toward you. He really doted on you, did things for you, communicated with you. On the surface, life with Jeff seemed pretty good.

"Remember, though, this didn't fit your picture of yourself—your belief about yourself. According to your belief, you shouldn't have a man who shows you this much love. You are not enough, remember?"

Jill nodded but still looked uncertain and rather perplexed.

"Your soul knows you must heal that belief, so it colludes with Jeff's soul somehow to bring it to your awareness. On the surface it seems that Jeff begins to act strangely and totally out of character. He then taunts you by loving another Lorraine, thus acting out with you the very same scenario you had with your father many years ago. He appears to be persecuting you mercilessly, and you feel totally helpless and victimized.

"Does this describe, more or less, your current situation?" I asked.

"I guess so," Jill said quietly. She wrinkled her brow as she tried to hold on to the new picture of her situation slowly forming in her mind.

"Well, here you are again, Jill, about to make a choice. You must choose whether to heal and grow—or to be right," I said and smiled. "If you make the choice people normally make, you will choose to be the victim and make Jeff wrong, which in turn will allow you to be right. After all, his behavior seems quite cruel and unreasonable, and I don't doubt there are many women who would support you in taking some drastic action in response to it. Haven't most of your friends been saying you should leave him?"

"Yes. Everyone says I should get out of the marriage if he doesn't change. I actually thought you would say that too," she added with a tinge of disappointment.

"A few years ago, I probably would have. But since my introduction to these spiritual principles, my whole way of looking at such situations has changed, as you can see," I said with a wry smile, looking across at John. He grinned but said nothing.

I continued. "So as you might guess, the other choice might be to recognize that beneath what seems to be happening on the surface, something else much more meaningful—and potentially very supportive—is going on. The other choice is to accept that Jeff's behavior may contain another message, another meaning or intent, and that within the situation lies a gift for you."

Jill thought for a while, then said, "Jeff's behavior is so darn bizarre, you'd have a hard time coming up with any good reason for it. Maybe something else is going on that I don't yet see. I suppose it's similar to what Henry was doing, but it's hard for me to see it with Jeff because I'm so confused right now. I can't see beyond what is actually going on."

"That's okay," I said, reassuring her. "Look, there's no need to figure it out. Just being willing to entertain the idea that something else is going on is a giant step forward. In fact, the willingness to see the situation differently is the key to your healing. Ninety percent of the healing occurs when you become willing to let in the idea that your soul has lovingly created this situation for you. In becoming willing, you let go of control and surrender it to God. He takes care of the other 10 percent. If you can really understand at a deep level and surrender to the idea that God will handle this for you if you turn it over to him, you won't need to do anything at all. The situation and your healing will both get handled automatically.

"But prior even to this step, you can take a perfectly rational step that enables you to see things differently right away. It involves separating fact from fiction. It means recognizing that your belief has no factual basis whatsoever. It is simply a story you have made up, based on a few facts and a whole lot of interpretation.

"We do this all the time: experience an event and make interpretations about it. Then we put these two pieces together to create a largely false story about what happened. The story becomes the belief, and we defend it as if it were the truth. It never is, of course.

"In your case, the facts were that Dad didn't hug you, didn't spend time playing with you, didn't hold you, didn't put you on his lap. He did not meet your needs for affection. Those were the facts. On the basis of those facts, you made a crucial assumption: 'Dad doesn't love me.' Isn't that true?"

She nodded.

"But the fact that he didn't meet your needs doesn't mean that he didn't love you. That's an interpretation. It wasn't true. He was a sexually repressed man, and intimacy was scary for him; we know that. Maybe he just didn't know how to express his love in the way you wanted to receive it. Do you remember that super doll-house he made you one year for Christmas? I remember him spending countless hours on it in the evenings when you were in bed. Perhaps that was the only way he knew how to express his love for you.

"I'm not making excuses for him or trying to make what you have said, or felt, wrong. I'm just trying to point out how we all make the mistake of thinking that our interpretations represent the truth.

"The next big assumption you made," I continued, "based on the facts and your first interpretation that 'Dad doesn't love me,' was 'It's my fault. There must be something wrong with me.' That was an even greater lie than the other assumption, don't you agree?"

She nodded.

"It isn't surprising that you would come to that conclusion, because that's the way little kids think. Since they perceive that the world revolves around them, they always assume that when things don't go well, it's their fault. When a child first thinks this, the thought is coupled with great pain. To reduce the pain, a child represses it, but this action actually makes it all the harder to get rid of the thought. Thus we stay stuck with the idea that 'It's my fault and something must be wrong with me' even as adults.

"Any time a situation in our life triggers the memory of this pain or the idea attached to it, we emotionally regress. Thus we feel and behave like the little kid who first experienced the pain. In fact, that's precisely what happened when you saw my Lorraine cause our father to feel love. You were twenty-seven years old, but at that moment you regressed to the two-year-old Jill who felt unloved and acted out all your childhood neediness. And you are still doing it, only this time you are doing it with your husband.

"The idea upon which you based all your relationships represents an interpretation made by a two-year-old kid and has absolutely no basis in fact," I concluded. "Do you see that, Jill?"

"Yes, I do. I made some pretty silly decisions based on those unconscious assumptions, didn't I?"

"Yes, you did, but you made them when you were in pain and when you were too young to know any better. Even though you repressed the pain to get rid of it, the belief kept working in your life at a subconscious level. That's when your soul decided to create some drama in your life so you would bring it to consciousness again and have the opportunity to choose healing once more.

"You attracted people into your life who would confront you directly with your own pain and make

you relive the original experience through them," I
continued. "That's what Jeff is doing right now. Of
course, I am not saying he is doing this consciously. He
really isn't. He is probably more perplexed by his own
behavior than you are. Remember, this is a soul-to-soul
transaction. His soul knows about your original pain
and is aware that you will not heal it without going
through the experience again."

"Wow!" Jill said, and took a deep breath. Her body
relaxed for the first time since we had begun talking
about the situation. "It's certainly a totally different
way of looking at things, but do you know what? I feel
lighter. It's as if a weight has been lifted off my shoul-
ders just by talking it through with you."

"That's because your energy has shifted," I replied.
"Imagine how much of your life-force energy you have
had to expend just keeping the story about Dad and
Lorraine alive. Plus, imagine the amount of energy
required to keep down the feelings of grief and resentment wrapped around the story. The tears you shed
earlier enabled you to release a lot of that. And you
have just acknowledged that it was all a made-up story
anyway—what a relief that must be. Also, you've had a
lot of energy locked up around Jeff—making him wrong,
making yourself wrong, being a victim, and so on. Just
being willing to see the whole situation differently

enables you to release all that energy and allow it to move through you. No wonder you feel lighter!"

"What would have happened if, instead of understanding what was going on underneath the situation with Jeff, I had simply left him?" Jill asked.

"Your soul would have brought in someone else to help you heal," I quickly replied. "But you didn't leave him, did you? You came here instead. You have to understand, this trip was no accident. There are no such things as accidents in this system. You—or rather, your soul—created this trip, this opportunity to understand the dynamics of the situation with Jeff. Your soul guided you here. John's soul created a trip at this particular time to make it possible for you to come with him."

"And what about the two Lorraines?" Jill wondered. "How did that happen? Surely, that's just a coincidence."

"There are no coincidences in this system either. Just know that your souls, and the souls of some others, conspired to create this situation, and notice how perfect it was that a person named Lorraine was involved in the original occasion and in this one. It couldn't have been a more perfect clue. It's hard to imagine that it wasn't set up somehow, don't you agree?" I said.

"So what do I do with this now?" asked Jill. "It's true that I feel lighter, but what do I do when I go home and see Jeff?"

"There really is very little for you to do," I answered. "From this point on, it's more a question of how you feel inside yourself. Do you understand that you are no longer a victim? Do you understand that Jeff is no longer a persecutor? Do you see that the situation was exactly what you needed and wanted? Do you feel how much that man loves you—at the soul level, I mean?"

"What do you mean?" Jill asked.

"He was willing to do whatever it took to get you to the point where you could look again at your belief about yourself and see that it was untrue. Do you realize how much discomfort he was willing to endure to help you? He is not a cruel man by nature, so it must have been hard for him. Few men could have done that for you while risking losing you in the process. Jeff, or Jeff's soul, truly is an angel for you. When you really understand this, you will feel so grateful to him! Plus, you will stop sending out messages that you are unlovable. You will have the ability to let love in, perhaps for the first time in your life. You will have forgiven Jeff, because you will be clear that nothing wrong ever took place. It was perfect in every sense.

"And I promise you this," I continued. "Jeff is already changing and dropping his bizarre behavior as we speak. His soul is already picking up that you have forgiven him and healed your misperception about yourself. As you change your energy, his energy changes too. You're connected energetically. Physical distance is irrelevant."

Getting back to her question, I said, "So, you won't have to do anything special when you get home. In fact, I want you to promise me that you won't do anything at all when you get back. In particular, do not, under any circumstances, share with Jeff this new way of looking at the situation. I want you to see how everything will be different *automatically simply as a consequence of you changing your perception.*

"You will feel changed as well," I added. "You will find yourself feeling more peaceful, more centered, and more relaxed. You will have a knowingness that will seem strange to Jeff for a while. It will take time for your relationship with him to adjust, and it may still be difficult for a while, but this issue will resolve now," I concluded with conviction.

Jill and I reviewed this new way of looking at her situation many times before she returned home to England. It is always difficult for someone in the middle of an emotional upset to shift into a Radical Forgiveness perspective. In fact, getting to a place where Radical Forgiveness can truly happen often requires a great deal of integration and repetitive reinforcement. To help my sister, I introduced her to some breathing techniques that help to release emotion and integrate new ways of being and asked her to complete a Radical Forgiveness worksheet. (See Part Four, "Tools for Radical Forgiveness.")

The day she left, Jill was obviously nervous about going back to the situation she had left behind. As she walked down the jetway to her airplane, she looked back and tried to wave confidently, but I knew she was scared that she might lose her newfound understanding and get drawn back into the drama.

Apparently the meeting with Jeff went well. Jill requested that he not question her immediately about what had happened while she was away. She also requested that he give her space for a few days in order to get settled. But she immediately noticed a difference in him. He was attentive, kind, and considerate—more like the Jeff she had known before this whole episode began.

Over the next couple of days, Jill told Jeff she no longer blamed him for anything, nor did she want him to change in any way. She said she had learned that it was she who needed to take responsibility for her own feelings and that she would deal with whatever came up for her in her own way without making him wrong. She did not elaborate at all and did not try to explain herself.

Things went well for some days after Jill's return home, and Jeff's behavior with his daughter Lorraine changed dramatically. In fact, everything seemed to be getting back to normal with regard to that relationship, but the atmosphere between Jeff and Jill remained tense and their communication limited.

About two weeks later, the situation came to a head. Jill looked at Jeff and said quietly, "I feel like I've lost my best friend."

"So do I," he replied.

For the first time in months they connected. They hugged each other and began to cry. "Let's talk," Jill said. "I've got to tell you what I learned with Colin in America. It's going to sound weird to you at first, but I want to share it with you. You don't have to believe it. I just want you to hear me. Are you willing?"

"I'll do whatever it takes," Jeff replied. "I know something important happened to you there. I want to know what it was. You have changed, and I like what I see. You are not the same person you were when you stepped on the airplane with John. So tell me what happened."

Jill talked and talked. She explained the dynamics of Radical Forgiveness as best she could in a way Jeff could understand. She felt strong and powerful—sure of herself and her understanding, secure and clear in her mind.

Jeff, a practical man who is always skeptical of anything that cannot be rationally explained, did not resist this time, and he was indeed quite receptive to the ideas Jill asked him to consider. He voiced openness to the idea that there might be a spiritual world beneath everyday reality and, given that, saw a certain logic in the Radical Forgiveness concept. He didn't accept it totally, but he nevertheless was willing to listen, consider, and see how it had changed Jill.

After the discussion, they both felt their love had been rekindled and that their relationship had a good chance of surviving. They made no promises, though, and agreed to keep talking to each other while they watched how their relationship progressed.

It did, indeed, progress quite well. Jeff still fawned over his daughter Lorraine to a degree, but not as much as before. Jill found she cared hardly at all even when he did behave in this manner. It certainly did not trigger her to regress emotionally and react from old beliefs about herself.

Within a month of their conversation about Radical Forgiveness, all of Jeff's past behavioral pattern with Lorraine stopped. In turn, Lorraine didn't call or visit as often; she got on with her life. Everything slowly returned to normal and Jill and Jeff's relationship began to grow more secure and loving than ever before. Jeff became the kind, sensitive man he is by nature, Jill became less needy, and Lorraine became much happier.

Looking back, had Jill's soul not brought her to Atlanta to create the opportunity for us to have our conversation, I feel sure she and Jeff would have separated. In the grand scheme of things, that would have been all right too. Jill simply would have found someone else with whom to recreate the drama and another opportunity to heal. As it was, she took this opportunity to heal and stayed in the relationship.

At the time of writing this second edition, many years after that crisis, they remain together and are very happily married. Like every other couple, they continue to create dramas in their lives—but they know now how to see them as healing opportunities and move through them quickly and with grace.

*Note: The time-line diagram on the next page depicts Jill's story as a graphic. She found this helped her greatly to see how the original pain of not feeling loved by her father had led to a belief that she was not enough and how, in turn, that belief had played out in her life. You might do the same for yourself if you think you have a similar story running your life.*

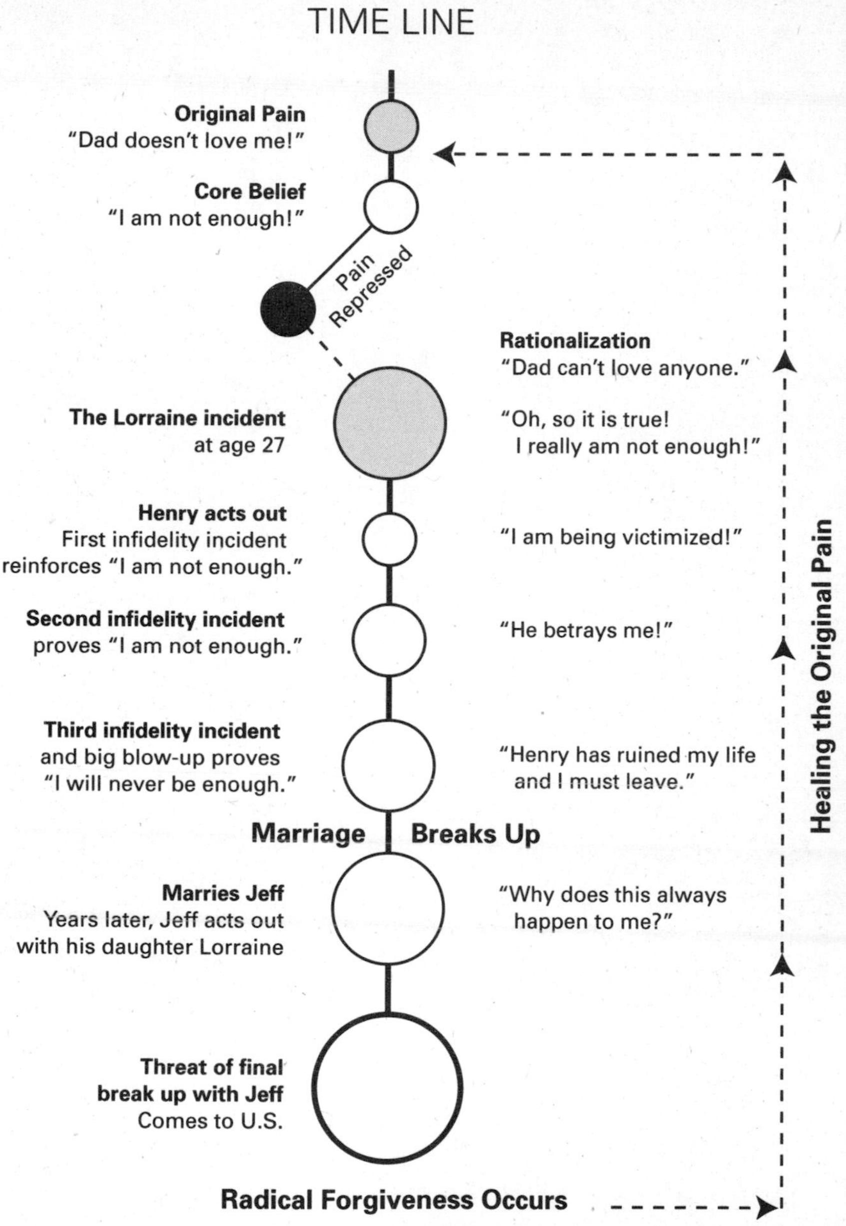

# TIME LINE

**Original Pain**
"Dad doesn't love me!"

**Core Belief**
"I am not enough!"

Pain Repressed

**The Lorraine incident**
at age 27

**Rationalization**
"Dad can't love anyone."

"Oh, so it is true!
I really am not enough!"

**Henry acts out**
First infidelity incident
reinforces "I am not enough."

"I am being victimized!"

**Second infidelity incident**
proves "I am not enough."

"He betrays me!"

**Third infidelity incident**
and big blow-up proves
"I will never be enough."

"Henry has ruined my life
and I must leave."

**Marriage   Breaks Up**

**Marries Jeff**
Years later, Jeff acts out
with his daughter Lorraine

"Why does this always
happen to me?"

**Threat of final
break up with Jeff**
Comes to U.S.

**Radical Forgiveness Occurs**

Healing the Original Pain

FIGURE 1   **Jill's Healing Journey**

# part two

# Conversations on Radical Forgiveness

# 2  Underlying Assumptions

SINCE ALL THEORIES are based upon certain assumptions, it is important to have an understanding of the spiritual assumptions underlying the theory and practice of Radical Forgiveness. Before looking at these, though, it is worth noting that even the most widely accepted scientific theories are often based on assumptions for which there is very little hard evidence.

We can say the same thing about the basic assumptions handed down throughout the ages about God, human nature, and the spiritual realm. While there is little hard scientific evidence to support their validity, such assumptions have been handed down to us as universal truths, or principles, for centuries, and have formed the foundation for many great spiritual traditions throughout the world. They certainly are foundational to Radical Forgiveness. Some of these assumptions are now being proven by physicists to be scientifically well founded.

I prefer to use the word "assumption" rather than "belief" or even "principle" because simply classifying an idea as an assumption allows for the possibility of a greater truth emerging in the future. I am more likely to be open to seeing the deeper meaning in something if I am not ego-invested in a belief system I feel obliged to defend. I prefer to hang out in the question rather than take a fixed position on something that has yet to be proven.

I have also discovered that the process of Radical Forgiveness works equally well whether you believe in it or not. So long as you are willing to try it and use the tools the system provides, it seems to work. Belief is not necessary.

In any case, Radical Forgiveness makes very little sense to the rational mind, at least to that part of the mentality that is grounded in everyday reality as perceived through the five senses. That's because Radical Forgiveness operates according to spiritual law, not physical law. It is essentially a metaphysical idea.

Nevertheless, in order to wrap our minds around the basic idea as best we can, it helps to go over some of the assumptions that give some structure to the concept and a quasi-rational basis for understanding the technology.

Each assumption listed here is expanded upon at length in various other places in the book. They are as follows:

- We have bodies that die, but we have immortal souls that existed prior to our incarnation and continue to exist after death. (Therefore, death is an illusion.)

- While our bodies and our senses tell us we are separate individuals, we are all one. We all individually vibrate as part of a single whole.

- In order to exponentially expand our awareness of oneness, we agreed to come to this world of duality in order to experience the exact opposite of oneness—separation.

- Part of the agreement was that we would forget the world of oneness we came from in order to fully experience the pain of separation. When we have experienced the amount of pain we agreed to have in this lifetime, we use Radical Forgiveness to awaken and remember who we are.

- Since the pain of separation is an emotional experience, we need a body to be able to feel it.

- The human experience is meant to be an emotional one, so the extent to which we deny our feelings is the extent to which we deny our purpose for being here.

- We are spiritual beings having a spiritual experience in human bodies.

- Vibrationally, we live in two worlds simultaneously:
    1. The World of Divine Truth (Spirit)
    2. The World of Humanity
  Once we awaken, we can live comfortably in both.

- The World of Humanity is a spiritual classroom, and life is the curriculum. Our lessons are the events that happen in life. The objective is to awaken to the truth of who we are and return home.

- When we decided to incarnate into the World of Humanity, God gave us total free will to live the experiment in any way we choose and to find for ourselves the way back home.

- We have three forms of intelligence: mental, emotional, and spiritual. Our spiritual intelligence knows the truth of who we are and connects us directly to universal intelligence.

- Life is not random. It provides for the purposeful unfoldment of our own divine plan, with opportunities to make choices and decisions in every moment guided by our Higher Self and ego.

- There are two definitions of the ego. The first sees it as our friend and loving guide, while the second casts it as our enemy. They are as follows:
    1. A part of our soul whose job it is, in cahoots with our Higher Self and our spiritual intelligence, to lovingly find all sorts of ways for us to experience the pain of separation, that being the purpose for our being on the earth plane.
    2. An insidious, deep-seated subconscious guilt complex based on our belief that we

committed the original sin of separating from God, who will eventually punish us for doing so. The ego seeks every way possible to reinforce itself and blocks any attempt to reveal the truth that we never separated from God at all. It cleverly ensures its survival by "protecting" us from our overwhelming guilt, as well as the fear of God's wrath, through the mechanisms of repression and projection. (See Chapter 7.)

- We create our reality through the Law of Cause and Effect. Thoughts are causes that show up in our world as physical effects. Reality is an outplaying of our consciousness. Our world offers a mirror of our beliefs. (See Chapter 9.)

- At the soul level, we get precisely what we need in our lives for our spiritual growth. How we judge what we get determines whether we experience life as painful or joyful.

- Through relationship we grow and learn. Through relationship we heal and are returned to wholeness and truth. We need others to mirror our misperceptions and our projections and to help us bring repressed material to consciousness for healing.

- Through the Law of Resonance, we attract people who resonate with our issues so that we can heal them. For example, if abandonment is our issue, we will tend to attract people who abandon us. In that sense, these people serve as our teachers. (See Chapter 8.)

- We come into the physical life experience with a mission: to fully experience a particular energy pattern so we can feel the feelings associated with that pattern and then transform that energy through love. (See Chapter 10.)

- Physical reality is an illusion created by our five senses. Matter consists of interrelating energy fields vibrating at different frequencies. (See Chapter 13.)

*Note: If you find yourself unable to accept any of these assumptions, simply disregard them. It will make no difference to the effectiveness of the Radical Forgiveness experience.*

# 3  Worlds Apart

WHAT WE MIGHT learn from Jill's story is that things are not always what they seem. What appears to be cruel and nasty behavior on somebody's part might be exactly what we need and have indeed called forth. Situations that appear to be the worst that could possibly befall us may hold the key to our healing something deep within us that keeps us from being happy and prevents our growth. The people who seem to us to be the most troublesome and the least likable may therefore be our greatest teachers. What we think they do *to* us, they actually do *for* us.

If I am right about this, then it follows that whatever appears to be happening is seldom what is truly occurring. Beneath the apparent circumstances of every situation exists a wholly different reality—a different world altogether; a world that we are not privy to except for the occasional glimpse.

Jill's story demonstrates this fact beautifully. On the surface, there was the drama of what was happening between her, Jeff, and his daughter Lorraine. It was not pretty. It looked as though Jeff was being cruel and insensitive. It was easy to identify Jill as a victim in the situation and Jeff as the villain. Yet there were enough clues to lead us to the possibility that something else of a more loving nature was happening, and that it was being orchestrated at the spiritual level.

As the story unfolded, it became obvious that Jill's soul was doing a dance with the souls of Jeff and Lorraine and that the situation being played out was purely for her soul's benefit. Moreover, far from being a villain, Jeff was actually a hero and, from that spiritual perspective, had done nothing wrong. He had simply played his part in the drama, as dictated by his soul, acting in support of Jill's growth at the soul level.

When we shift our perspective to this possibility, we become open to the idea that nothing wrong took place and that in fact there was nothing to forgive. This is precisely the notion that defines Radical Forgiveness. It is also what makes it radical.

If we had asked Jill to apply traditional forgiveness to this situation, we would not have investigated this "other world" possibility. We would have taken the evidence of our five senses and used our intellect to come to the conclusion that Jeff had wronged and badly treated her and that if she were to forgive him, she would have to accept what he did and try her best to let it go, or "let bygones be bygones."

From this we notice that traditional forgiveness takes it as a given that something wrong happened. Radical Forgiveness, on the other hand, takes the position that nothing wrong happened and that, consequently, there is nothing to forgive. We can put it like this:

With traditional forgiveness, the willingness to forgive is present but so is the residual need to condemn. Therefore victim consciousness is maintained and nothing changes.

With Radical Forgiveness, the willingness to forgive is present but not the need to condemn. Therefore, the victim consciousness is dropped, and everything changes.

("Victim consciousness" is defined as the conviction that someone else has done something bad to you, and, as a direct result, they are responsible for the lack of peace and happiness in your life.)

## DIFFERENT WORLDS—
## DIFFERENT PERSPECTIVES

Traditional forgiveness should not be seen as inferior to Radical Forgiveness. It is simply different. When used in the context of a certain set of beliefs—beliefs that

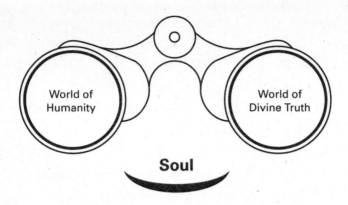

FIGURE 2   **The Existential Chain of Being**

are firmly rooted in the physical world and in everyday human reality—traditional forgiveness is the only form of forgiveness possible and has great value in its own right. It calls upon the finest of human qualities and characteristics, such as compassion, mercy, tolerance, humility, and kindness. Joan Borysenko calls forgiveness "the exercise of compassion."[1]

Radical Forgiveness is different from traditional forgiveness because it is rooted in the metaphysical reality of the world of Spirit—that which I call the World of Divine Truth.

This makes the distinction between radical and traditional forgiveness very clear, because we can see now that in each case we look through a completely different lens. The lens we are using to view a situation will determine whether we are using traditional forgiveness or Radical Forgiveness. Each provides us with a completely different point of view.

But we should not fall into the trap of thinking of it in terms of either/or. It is a both/and situation. This is because we live with one foot in each world (since we are spiritual beings having a human experience) and can therefore reference situations through either lens or both lenses at the same time. While being fully grounded in the World of Humanity, we remain connected to the World of Divine Truth through our soul.

Since the importance of the distinction between these two worlds cannot be overemphasized, some further explanation will be helpful here.

The World of Humanity and the World of Divine Truth represent two ends of a vibrational scale. When we vibrate at a low frequency, our bodies become dense and we exist only in the World of Humanity. When we vibrate at a high level, which makes our bodies become lighter, we exist also in the World of Divine Truth. Depending upon our vibration at any moment, we move up and down the scale toward one world or the other.

The World of Humanity represents the world of objective reality we see as "outside ourselves." As a

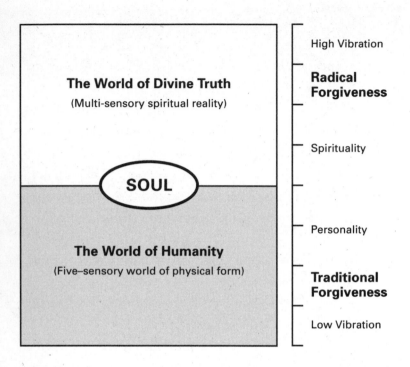

FIGURE 3 **Perspectives on Two Worlds**

world of form, it provides the setting in which we live our everyday human lives, as well as the reality we experience through our five senses. It holds the energy patterns of death, change, fear, limitation, and duality. This world provides us with the environment in which we, as spiritual beings, can experience being human. This means having a physical body and working with (and possibly transcending) a particular energy pattern associated with the World of Humanity that we may have specifically "come in" to work with. The World of Divine Truth, on the other hand, has no physical form and already carries the energy pattern of eternal life, immutability, infinite abundance, love, and one-ness with God. Even though we cannot perceive this world with our senses, and we scarcely possess the mental capacity to comprehend it, we can get enough of a sense of it to know that it is real. Such activities as prayer, meditation, and Radical Forgiveness, all of which raise our vibration, allow us to access the World of Divine Truth.

These existential realms differ not in terms of place or time but solely in their vibrational level. The study of quantum physics has proven that all reality con-sists of energy patterns and that consciousness sustains these energy patterns. Thus, the world of form exists as dense concentrations of energy vibrating at frequencies we can experience through our physical senses. On the other hand, we experience the World of Divine Truth as an inner knowing and an extrasensory awareness.

Because these two worlds exist on the same cont-inuum, we do not live sometimes in one and sometimes in the other. We live in both worlds at the same time. However, which world we experience at any given moment depends upon our awareness of them and how awake we are. Obviously, as human beings our consciousness resonates easily with the World of Humanity. Our senses naturally pull us into that world and convince us that it is real. Though some people are less grounded in the world of objective reality than others, human beings, on the whole, are firmly entrenched at this end of the continuum—which is as it should be.

Our awareness of the World of Divine Truth is limited, and this, too, appears to be by design. Our soul enters into this world to experience being human—thus our memory and awareness of the World of Divine Truth must be limited in order to allow us the full experience. We would not be able to take on fully the energies of separation, change, fear, death, limitation, and duality that characterize this world if we knew they were illusory. If we incarnated with this memory, we would deny ourselves the opportunity to transcend these states and to discover that they are, indeed, simply illusions. By forgetting who we are when we take on a physical body, we give ourselves the chance to experience fully the pain of separation—that is, until we begin to awaken and remember once more the truth of who we are.

During a gathering in Atlanta in 1990, I heard Gerald Jampolsky, a well-known author, tell a true story about a couple returning home from the hospital after giving birth to their second child. It is a story that illustrates the fact that we have a true knowing of our connection with God and our own soul, but that we forget it fairly quickly after taking on a body. The couple were conscious of the need to include their three-year-old daughter in the celebration of the new baby's homecoming. But they felt perturbed by her insistence that she be allowed to go alone into the room with the baby. To honor her request yet oversee the situation, they switched on the baby monitor so they could at least hear what was going on, if not see it. What they heard astounded them. The little girl went straight to the crib, looked through the bars at the newborn child, and said, "Baby, tell me about God. I'm beginning to forget."

In spite of the veil we lower over the memory of our oneness with God, which the above story suggests might become fully drawn around the age of three, as humans we are not denied a connection to the World of Divine Truth. Our soul carries a vibration that resonates with the World of Divine Truth and connects us to that world. We can aid this connection through practices like meditation, prayer, yoga, breathwork, dancing, and chanting. Through such practices, we raise our vibration enough to resonate with that of the World of Divine Truth.

There is evidence to suggest that even this is changing rapidly. Everywhere I go, I ask the same question of my workshop participants: "How many of you are aware of a quickening or a speed-up in our spiritual evolution—and that we are being asked by Spirit to move more quickly through our lessons in preparation for a profound shift of some kind?" There is almost unanimous concurrence. More and more people now talk openly and freely about always being in touch with their "guidance" and are willing to trust it more each day. The veil between the two worlds is definitely becoming thinner. Radical Forgiveness contributes to this process both at the individual level and at the level of collective awareness.

Yet the two types of forgiveness remain literally worlds apart. Each demands a different way of looking at the world and at life. Clearly, traditional forgiveness offers itself as a way of living in the world, while Radical Forgiveness is nothing less than a spiritual path.

In terms of our capacity to evolve spiritually, Radical Forgiveness offers extraordinary potential to transform consciousness, and this potential far exceeds what is possible with traditional forgiveness. Yet we must recognize that we all still live in the World of Humanity, and at certain times we will fall short of what we might

| TRADITIONAL FORGIVENESS | vs. | RADICAL FORGIVENESS |
|---|---|---|
| World of Humanity (Ego) | vs. | World of Divine Truth (Spirit) |
| Low vibratory rate | vs. | High vibratory rate |
| Something wrong happened | vs. | Nothing wrong happened |
| Judgment based | vs. | Judgment and blame free |
| Past time orientation | vs. | Present time orientation |
| Need to figure it all out | vs. | Surrendering to what is, as is |
| Victim consciousness | vs. | Grace consciousness |
| Judges human imperfection | vs. | Accepts human imperfection |
| What happened did (true) | vs. | Symbolic meaning of it (truth) |
| Physical reality only | vs. | Metaphysical realities |
| Problem is still "out there" | vs. | Problem is with me (my error) |
| Letting go of resentment | vs. | Embracing the resentment |
| You and I are separate | vs. | You and I are ONE |
| "Shit happens" | vs. | There are no accidents |
| Life is random events | vs. | Life is purposeful |
| Personality (ego) in control | vs. | Soul following a divine plan |
| Reality is what happens | vs. | Reality is what we create |
| Death is real | vs. | Death is an illusion |

FIGURE 4 **Distinctions Between Traditional and Radical Forgiveness.** For more explanation of these distinctions, see Chapter 15: Articles of Faith.

57

think of as the spiritual ideal. When we find ourselves immersed in pain, for example, it becomes virtually impossible for us to move into Radical Forgiveness. When we have recently experienced harm at the hand of another, such as being raped, we cannot be expected to accept, in that moment, that the experience was something we wanted and that it represents the unfolding of a divine plan. We will not have the receptivity necessary to entertain that idea. It can only come later, in moments of quiet reflection, not in the heat of anger or in the immediate aftermath of trauma.

Then again, we must continually remind ourselves that what we have created *is* the spiritual ideal; that we have created circumstances in our lives that help us to grow and learn; that the lessons we need to learn are contained in the situation; and that the only way to obtain the growth from the experience is to go *through* it.

Our choice in this is not so much whether or not to have the experience (Spirit decides this for us), but how long we are going to hang out in victim consciousness because of it. Should we choose to quickly let go of victimhood, it is comforting to know that we have a technology that will make that happen. Traditional forgiveness, by contrast, has little to offer in this regard.

## *Summary*

- Traditional forgiveness is firmly rooted in the World of Humanity. In the same way that the World of Humanity holds the energy of duality, so traditional forgiveness polarizes and judges everything as either good or bad, right or wrong.

  *Radical Forgiveness takes the view that there is no right/wrong or good/bad. Only our thinking makes it so.*

- Traditional forgiveness always begins with the assumption that something wrong took place and someone "did something" to someone else. The victim archetype remains operative.

  *Radical Forgiveness begins with the belief that nothing wrong happened and there are no victims in any situation.*

- Traditional forgiveness is effective to the extent that it calls upon the highest human virtues, such as compassion, tolerance, kindness, mercy, and humility. These qualities point toward forgiveness and have healing potential. However, in and of themselves, they are not forgiveness.

*Radical Forgiveness is no different in this regard, since it also calls for these same virtues to be present in the process.*

• Traditional forgiveness depends entirely upon our own capacity to feel compassion, so it is limited in this regard. No matter how much compassion or tolerance we muster for someone like Hitler, and no matter how much we empathize with the pain of his upbringing, nothing enables us to forgive him (using traditional forgiveness) for the mass murder of over 13 million people.

*Radical Forgiveness has no limits whatsoever and is completely unconditional. If Radical Forgiveness cannot forgive Hitler, it can forgive nobody. Like unconditional love, it's all or nothing.*

• With traditional forgiveness, the ego and our personality-self call the shots. Hence, the

problem always appears "out there" with
someone else.

*With Radical Forgiveness, the finger points the
other way. The problem lies "in here," with me.*

• Traditional forgiveness believes in the reality
of the physical world, in the complete integrity
of "what happens"; it always tries to "figure it
all out" and thus control the situation.

*Radical Forgiveness recognizes the illusion,
sees that what happened was just a story, and
responds by surrendering to the perfection of
the situation.*

• Traditional forgiveness does not factor in the
notion of a spiritual mission and maintains its
belief in, and fear of, death.

*Radical Forgiveness sees death as an illusion
and takes the view that life is eternal.*

• Traditional forgiveness views life as a problem
to be solved or punishment to be avoided. It
experiences life as a random set of circumstances

that just happen to us for no reason—thus, the popular bumper sticker, "Shit happens!"

*Radical Forgiveness sees life as entirely purposeful and motivated by love.*

• Traditional forgiveness recognizes the inherent imperfection of human beings but fails to see the *perfection in the imperfection.* It cannot resolve that paradox.

*Radical Forgiveness exemplifies that paradox.*

• Traditional forgiveness can carry a high vibration similar to Radical Forgiveness when calling upon some of the highest of human virtues, like kindness, humility, compassion, patience, and tolerance.

*The portal through which we begin the journey of raising our vibration to connect with the world of Divine Truth and experience Radical Forgiveness is the open heart.*

• Traditional forgiveness, when of a very high vibration, recognizes the profundity of the

spiritual insight that we all are imperfect and
that imperfection characterizes the nature
of humanity. When we look at a wrongdoer
through these eyes, we can say in all humility
and with tolerance and compassion, "There
but for the Grace of God, go I." We own that
we, too, are completely capable of whatever the
accused person has done. If we are acquainted
with our shadow self, we know that we all
have within us the potential to cause harm,
to murder, to rape, to abuse children, and to
annihilate 13 million people. This knowledge
allows us to call forth our humility and makes
us kind and merciful not only to the accused
but to ourselves, for in them we recognize our
own inherent imperfection, our own shadow.
This recognition brings us very close to actually
taking back that which we projected—the vital
first step in Radical Forgiveness.

*Radical Forgiveness also lovingly sees the*
*imperfection inherent in human beings, but*
*sees the perfection in the imperfection.*

- Radical Forgiveness recognizes that forgiveness
  cannot be willed or bestowed. We must be

willing to forgive and to give the situation over to our Higher Power. Forgiveness of any kind comes not from effort but from being open to experiencing it.

## WHAT IS *NOT* FORGIVENESS

While we are dealing with definitions, we should also be clear about what is *not* forgiveness. A lot of what passes for forgiveness is what I call "pseudo-forgiveness."

Lacking authenticity, pseudo-forgiveness is usually just neatly packaged judgment and concealed resentment masquerading as forgiveness. The willingness to forgive is not there, and, far from decreasing victim consciousness, it actually expands it. However, the line between this and traditional forgiveness may not be easy to determine.

### *Examples of Pseudo-Forgiveness*

The following examples are listed in order of descending clarity, beginning with those that are obviously false and ending with those that come close to traditional forgiveness.

- **Forgiving out of a sense of obligation.** This is completely inauthentic, yet many of us forgive from this place. We think of forgiveness as the right thing or even the spiritual thing to do. We think we *ought* to forgive.

- **Forgiving out of a sense of righteousness.** This is the antithesis of forgiveness. If you forgive people because you think you are right and they are stupid, or because you pity them, that is pure arrogance.

- **Bestowing forgiveness or pardoning.** This is pure self-delusion. We do not possess the power to bestow forgiveness on anyone. When we bestow forgiveness, we play God. Forgiveness is not something we control—it just happens when we are willing.

- **Pretending forgiveness.** Pretending that we are not angry about something when we actually are angry provides not so much an opportunity to forgive as an opportunity to deny our anger. This represents a form of self-invalidation. When we do this, we allow others to treat us like the proverbial doormat. Such behavior usually stems from a fear of not forgiving, of being abandoned, or from a belief that expressing anger is unacceptable.

- **Forgive and forget.** This simply creates denial. Forgiveness is never simple erasure. Wise people forgive but *do not* forget. They strive to appreciate the gift inherent in the situation and to remember the lesson it taught them.

- **Making excuses.** When we forgive, we often do it with explanations or by making excuses for the person we are forgiving. For example, we might say about our parents, "My father abused me because he was abused by his own parents. He was doing the best he could." Forgiveness should be about letting go of the past and refusing to be controlled by it. If an explanation helps one to let go, it may be helpful to that extent, though an explanation does not remove the idea that something wrong happened. Therefore, at best, it can only be traditional forgiveness. It also possesses a certain righteousness, which may mask anger. On the other hand, understanding why someone did what they did and having empathy for them connects us again to our own imperfection and opens the door to feeling compassion and mercy— leading to a higher vibration of traditional

forgiveness but still falling short of
Radical Forgiveness.

- **Forgiving the person but not condoning the behavior.** This largely intellectual approach may only masquerade as forgiveness, because it remains judgmental and self-righteous. It also has practical and semantic problems. How do you separate a murderer from the act of murder?

This last one raises the issues of accountability and responsibility, both of which are the subject of the next chapter.

# 4 Accountability

IT MUST BE clearly understood that Radical Forgiveness does not relieve us from responsibility in this world. We are spiritual beings having a human experience in a world governed by both physical and man-made laws, and as such we are necessarily held to account for all our actions. That is an inherent part of the human experience that cannot be avoided.

In other words, when we create circumstances that hurt other people, we must accept that in the World of Humanity there are consequences for such actions. While from a Radical Forgiveness standpoint we would say that all parties involved in the situation are getting what they need, it is also true that experiencing the consequences, like going to jail or being fined, shamed, or condemned, is all part of the lesson and is perfect once again in that spiritual context.

I am often asked whether, in a situation where someone has done us harm and where the normal reaction would be to seek redress through the courts, a forgiving person would actually take that course of action. The answer is yes. We live in the World of Humanity, which operates within the parameters of the Law of Cause and Effect. This states that for every action there is a corresponding equal reaction. Thus, early on we learn that our actions have consequences. If we were never held accountable for our actions, forgiveness would be meaningless and valueless. With no accountability demanded of us, it would appear as if, no matter what we did, no one would care. Such an action or attitude offers no compassion whatsoever. For instance, children always interpret *rightful* parental discipline applied appropriately as caring and loving. Conversely, they interpret being given total license by their parents as non-caring. Children know.

However, the extent to which we respond to other people's actions with a sense of righteous indignation, grievance, revenge, and resentment rather than with a genuine desire to balance the scales with regard to principles of fairness, freedom, and respect for others determines our level of forgiveness. Righteousness and revenge lower our vibration. Conversely, defense of principles and acting with integrity raises our vibration. The higher the vibration, the closer we come to Divine Truth and the more able we are to forgive radically.

I recently heard bestselling author Alan Cohen tell a story that illustrates this point well. A friend of his once got involved in circumstances that resulted in a girl's death. For her wrongful death, he was imprisoned for many years. He accepted the responsibility for what had happened and behaved in every way as a model prisoner. Still, the girl's father, a rich and influential man with friends in high places, made a vow to keep this man locked up for as many years as possible. Every time he became eligible for parole, the girl's father spent a great deal of time and money pulling every political string possible to make sure parole was denied. After numerous such occurrences, Cohen asked his friend how he felt about being denied parole because of this man's efforts to keep him in prison. The man said he forgave the girl's father every day of his life and prayed for him, because he realized that it was the father who was in prison, not himself.

In truth, the father, who was unable to get beyond his rage, sadness, and grief, was controlled by his need for revenge. He could not escape the prison of his own victimhood. Even traditional forgiveness was beyond him. Cohen's friend, on the other hand, refused to be a victim and saw love as the only possibility. His vibration was higher, and he was able to practice Radical Forgiveness.

Getting back to the issue of whether or not to seek redress through the courts, yes, we should seek to make others accountable for their actions. Remember, though, that once we decide to sue, we must, as they say in Alcoholics Anonymous, "pray for the S.O.B."— and for ourselves. (By the way, we do not have to like someone in order to forgive him!) In other words, we turn the matter over to our Higher Power. We recognize that divine love operates in every situation and that each person receives exactly what he or she wants. We recognize that perfection always resides somewhere in the situation, even if it is not apparent at the time.

I had occasion to experience this myself when I had just completed this book and was looking around for someone to help me market it. A friend recommended someone, so my wife, JoAnn, and I went to see her. She seemed okay, and I had no reason to doubt her skill or integrity. However—it's funny how the Universe works—the deadline for getting the title into *Books in Print* was the following day. This is the reference book that bookstores use for ordering, "so it was important to get in then to avoid missing a whole year." That also meant I was rushed into signing a contract with this woman and coming up with $4,000, which is what she wanted up front, as well as 15 percent of the book sales.

We didn't have $4,000, but JoAnn somehow came up with $2,900; we would pay the rest in monthly installments. So we signed. Though rushed into it, I was pleased that I had delegated that part of the project.

As the months went by, and well after my book was published, I noticed that I was still having to do a lot of what I thought I had contracted with her to do. I was booking all my own signings, sending books to reviewers, and so on. I wasn't seeing any results from her efforts at all. I kept my eye on it, and after a while I confronted her. It turned out that she had hardly done a thing. Of course she denied it and defended herself, but when I demanded to see letters and evidence of activity, there was nothing. I fired her, voided the contract for nonperformance, and demanded my money back. Of course she refused, so I started court proceedings to recoup the money.

As you can imagine, I was pretty upset. I was stuck where all people who imagine themselves victimized go—in "Victimland!" And I was completely unconscious. I had my victim story all made up and took every opportunity to share it with anyone who would listen. As far as I was concerned, she had stolen that money from me, and I needed to get even. I was well and truly stuck, and I stayed that way for several weeks. And I was supposed to be Mr. Forgiveness!

Fortunately, a friend who had attended my first workshop many years before came to dinner. When I told her my story, her response was, "Well, have you done a worksheet around this?"

Of course I hadn't. It was the thing furthest from my mind. "No, I haven't done a worksheet," I replied, feeling very angry.

"Don't you think you should?" Lucie asked.

"No, I don't want to do a darn worksheet!" I shouted.

Then JoAnn chimed in. "Well, it's your worksheet. You ought to practice what you preach!" That did it. Feeling cornered, I stomped upstairs to get one, but I was angry. I knew, and so did they, that I was doing it under protest. It was the last thing in the world I wanted to do, but they wouldn't let me off the hook. I did each step in a huff and with little or no commitment to the process. Then all of a sudden, as I got about halfway through, I had to read this statement: "I release the need to blame and the need to be right." That was when it hit me. *The need to be right!* All of a sudden it flashed before me what I was trying to be right about. I had a core belief that I always had to do everything myself! I saw that this incident was just another playing out of that belief. All the other times I had unconsciously created being let down that way flashed before my eyes. I then saw and fully understood that this woman was supporting me in becoming acquainted with this toxic belief so that I could release it and open myself to greater abundance.

Suddenly, all my anger evaporated, and I saw how I had shut myself off from the very things I believed in and was teaching. I felt very ashamed—but at least I was conscious again. I could now see that this woman was an angel of healing for me, and I switched from feeling anger and resentment to feeling profound gratitude and love for her.

Besides being a wonderful awakening, this was a very powerful and humbling lesson in how easy it is to become unconscious about spiritual law and how quickly you can be sucked into a drama. It was also a great demonstration of how quickly I could separate from my true nature and from everything I knew to be true even after having once awakened to it. It was also a powerful reminder of why we need spiritual friends who will support us by not buying in to our victim story and being prepared to challenge us on it.

Now, the question you are probably asking is, having realized that she was a healing angel for me, did I cancel the court case against her? Well, I can tell you, I agonized over this.

I recognized that, even though I now saw the truth from the perspective of the World of Divine Truth, the situation itself was deeply grounded in the World of Humanity. I offered to go to mediation twice, and she refused on both occasions. So I went ahead with the court case, reasoning that her soul needed to have that experience; otherwise it would have taken her out of it when I suggested mediation. But I went into it with my heart open and with the intention that the right and perfect outcome would ensue. The court found in my favor, and I got a judgment against her for most of the $4,000. I never got the money, but that didn't matter. The point was that we had trusted the process and had done what seemed to be necessary at the time.

The truth is, it wouldn't have mattered which way I decided. Spirit could have sorted it out some other way, and it all would have worked out okay in the end—as it always does. The idea that our decisions matter in the overall scheme of things is just our ego trying to make us feel separate and special. The Universe has everything handled no matter what we decide. But how we make those decisions—whether from love or fear, greed or generosity, false pride or humility, dishonesty or integrity—matters to us personally, because each decision we make affects our vibration.

Another situation I am often asked to address is what to do when one becomes aware of a child being abused. The question raised is: if we assume that the child's spiritual growth is being supported by this experience, should we take action or not, since to interfere would be to deny the child's soul its growth experience? My answer is always that, as human beings, we must do what it is right according to our present awareness of right and wrong—as defined in human law. So we act accordingly while at the same time knowing that, in spiritual law, nothing wrong is taking place. Naturally, then, we would intervene. As human beings, we cannot do otherwise. But our intervention is not wrong or right either, because either way Spirit has it handled.

My reasoning is that if it were in the best interest of the child's soul for there to be no intervention, Spirit would arrange things in such a way as to prevent it. In other words, if I am not supposed to intervene, Spirit will keep me unaware of the situation. Conversely, if Spirit makes me aware of the situation, I assume it has no problem with my intervening. In the end, it is not even my decision.

When I do intervene, though, I do it free of judgment and the need to blame anyone. I just do it, knowing that the Universe set the whole thing up for a reason and that there is perfection in there somewhere.

# 5  Radical Forgiveness Therapy

THERE'S LITTLE ABOUT Jill's story that is unusual. The reality is, it could be anyone's story. In fact, since the publication of the first edition of this book in 1997, many thousands of people have written, called, or emailed me to say that they identify so much with it that they felt, while reading it, that it was their own personal story. For many of those who have read it, this compelling story has been the beginning of their healing, just as it was for Jill.

Insofar as it is typical of many apparent relationship problems, the story also provides a good example of how Radical Forgiveness can be applied to the quite ordinary problems of everyday life and demonstrates its viability as a radical alternative to traditional counseling and psychotherapy. This practice became known as Radical Forgiveness Therapy (RFT).

There is some irony in this, since it is a fundamental principle of Radical Forgiveness that, notwithstanding all evidence to the contrary, nothing wrong is happening and there is nothing to change. How can it therefore be therapy? After all, the main principle underlying Radical Forgiveness is that "Without exception, everything that happens to us is divinely guided, purposeful, and for our greater good."

The very notion of therapy implies that something is amiss and needs to be changed. When we go to a therapist, we expect our therapist to ask himself or herself these three basic questions:

1. What is wrong with this person or circumstance?
2. What caused him/her to become this way?
3. How can his/her problem be fixed?

Since none of these questions are applicable to Radical Forgiveness, how can Radical Forgiveness become a therapeutic modality? The answer lies in the way it worked for Jill.

You might recall that in the beginning of the story with Jill, I acted out of an implicit agreement with her that she really did have a problem, that Jeff was the basic cause of it, and that the only way to react to it was by trying to find a solution. For quite some time I went down this traditional road with her. Only when

I thought the time was right did I suggest a different (Radical Forgiveness) approach.

At that point, I had to make it very clear to her that I was shifting the conversation in an entirely different direction and using an alternate set of assumptions. More particularly, I was shifting to a new set of questions. These were:

1. What is perfect about what is occurring for her?
2. How is this perfection being revealed?
3. How can she shift her viewpoint in order to accept that there might be a certain perfection in her situation?

I can assure you that Jill's original perception of the situation with Jeff, and of all prior situations with her previous husband, certainly did not agree with with the idea of everything being perfect. Indeed, she felt that what had occurred was *self-evidently* wrong or bad. Most people would have agreed with her.

But, as we saw, the healing occurred for her only when she realized that, in fact, there was no right or wrong in any of the situations, that she was clearly not being victimized by anyone, and that, far from being her enemy, Jeff was her healing angel. She slowly began to see how at every moment divine guidance was helping her to heal an earlier misperception and a related false belief system that for years had prevented her from expressing her true self. Each situation, including what was happening with Jeff, was, on that basis, a gift of grace.

This actually makes RFT less a therapy and more a process of education. The therapist—or coach, as I prefer to call him or her—acts not so much out of a desire to fix someone as to enlighten him or her. Radical Forgiveness is a spiritual philosophy that has practical application to people's lives insofar as it gives them a spiritual perspective which they can apply, in the manner of self-help, to whatever problem or situation they are dealing with.

The divine plan is not fixed. At any point in the unfolding of one's plan, one always has choice. Radical Forgiveness helps people to shift their viewpoint and make new choices based on their insights.

Jill's story demonstrates how difficult it can be to make that shift in perception. Even with fairly obvious clues, it took a lot of discussion and processing of emotional pain before she became open to understanding a different interpretation. This was especially true of her former husband's infidelity.

Imagine how tough it might be to sell the idea of Radical Forgiveness to a Holocaust victim or someone who has just been raped or otherwise violently abused. Indeed, much of RFT's preliminary work involves creating a willingness to even look at the *possibility* of there being perfection in what happened. Even then, depending on the circumstances, developing such a receptivity can take time and almost always requires a great deal of emotional release work first. It is, nevertheless, possible. I can say this because I have seen people with horrendous stories make tremendous shifts in very short periods of time.

Yet it remains possible that some people may never get to the point where they become receptive; they simply may never get beyond their feelings of victimhood. On the other hand, those who do find themselves able to see, even for a moment, the perfection in their situation are empowered to release their feelings of victimhood and to become free. Jill was one of those.

Therein lies the power of this work, for, as we shall see in later chapters, releasing victimhood provides the key to health, personal power, and spiritual evolution. We have been addicted to the victim archetype for eons, and as we move into the Aquarian Age (the next two-thousand-year period of spiritual evolution), we must answer the call to let go of the past, release the victim archetype, and be more aware of life occurring in the moment.

There are some prerequisites, however, for doing so. First, the receptivity that Radical Forgiveness ultimately depends upon requires us to be open to seeing things from a spiritual standpoint. It references no particular religion and excludes none, but it does require at least a belief in a Higher Power or Higher Intelligence and the idea of a spiritual reality beyond our own physical world. A strictly atheistic viewpoint will not allow Radical Forgiveness to occur, nor RFT to work. We shall see that to make Radical Forgiveness a reality in our lives, we need to be comfortable with the idea that we can walk in both worlds simultaneously.

Having said that, Radical Forgiveness can be explained in nonthreatening terms and in such language as to honor all people's religious beliefs. It can be explained in ways that provide a fit with any existing belief system, thus allowing people to listen with comfort. Besides that, a substantial part of Radical Forgiveness Therapy does not depend upon mystical or esoteric ideas for its validity. Repression, denial, and projection all are concepts firmly rooted in psychological theory, and can be explained fully in scientific terms.

Mixing traditional therapy with RFT will not work. I cannot stress this enough. The questions and the assumptions underlying the two forms are just too different. Any therapist who adds RFT to his or her tool kit must first be aware of the distinctions between RFT and traditional therapy and be able to clearly differentiate them to a client, and, second, must work hard to keep them separated.

In the main, Radical Forgiveness Therapy is for people who are not in the least mentally sick—just needing some help in dealing with the issues of daily life. However, if a person has profound issues and deeply repressed pain with complex defense mechanisms in place, he or she may be referred to a qualified psychotherapist with a thorough understanding of how to apply RFT beneficially.

The technology of Radical Forgiveness is deceptively simple and yet amazingly effective as therapy for the soul—for individuals, groups, races, even countries. For example, I have held workshops for Jews and other persecuted people who hold the pain of their race or group, and I have witnessed amazing shifts in their consciousness. They have been able to let go of the collective pain, and in so doing, I believe, help heal the collective consciousness of that group going back many generations.

# 6 The Mechanisms of the Ego

IN MATTERS OF a spiritual nature, it is seldom long before the conversation turns to the ego. Radical Forgiveness is no exception, since the ego does seem to play a central role. So, what constitutes the ego and what role does it play in Radical Forgiveness? I think there are at least two ways of answering this question. The first casts the ego as our enemy, while the second sees it as our friend.

The ego-as-enemy viewpoint makes the ego responsible for keeping us separated from Source out of self-interest for its own survival. Consequently, the ego is our spiritual enemy and we are at war with it. Many spiritual disciplines take this as their central idea and demand that the ego must be dropped or transcended as a prerequisite for spiritual growth. The ego-as-friend model, in contrast, sees the ego as being the part of our own soul that acts as our loving guide for our human experience.

I prefer to think that there is truth in both of these ideas even though, at first blush, they seem to be incompatible. Let me explain each in turn as I have come to understand them for myself, so you can make up your own mind.

## 1. THE EGO AS THE ENEMY

In this model, the ego is said to exist as a deeply held set of beliefs about who we are in relationship to Spirit, having been formed when we experimented with the thought of separation from the Divine Source. In fact, we could say that the ego is the belief that separation actually occurred.

At the moment of separation, so the story goes, the ego caused us to believe that God became very angry about our experiment. This immediately created enormous guilt within us. The ego then elaborated on its story by telling us that God would get even and punish us severely for our great sin. So great were the guilt and terror created in us by the belief that this story was true that we had no choice but to repress these emotions deep in our unconscious minds. This spared us from conscious awareness of them.

This tactic worked quite well, yet we retained a great fear that the feelings might rise again. To remedy this problem, the ego developed a new belief—that the guilt

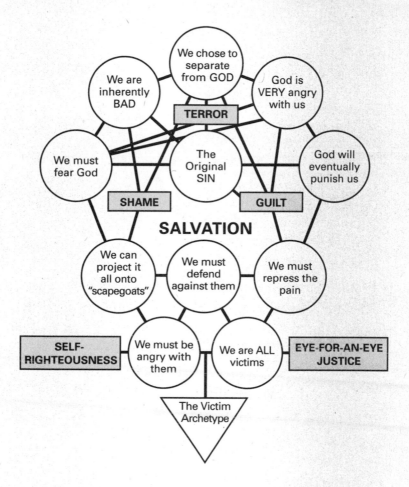

FIGURE 5   **The Structure of the Ego**

lay with someone else rather than within ourselves. In other words, we began projecting our guilt onto other people so we could be rid of it entirely. Others became our scapegoats. Then, to ensure that the guilt stayed with them, we became angry with them and continuously attacked them. (For more detailed information on denial and projection, see Chapter 7.)

Herein lies the origin of the victim archetype and the human race's continual need to attack and to defend against one another. After attacking the people onto whom we project our guilt, we fear they will attack us in return. So we create strong defenses to protect ourselves and what we see as our complete innocence. At some level we know we are guilty, so the more we defend against the attack, the more we reinforce our guilt. Thus we must constantly find people to hate, to criticize, to judge, to attack, and to make wrong simply so that we can feel better about ourselves. This dynamic constantly reinforces the ego's belief system, and in this manner, the ego ensures its own survival.

Using this behavior pattern as a reference, we can see why, throughout history, human beings have had such a high investment in their anger and such a great need to break the world into victims and persecutors, villains and heroes, victors and vanquished, winners and losers.

Furthermore, the perception we have of a we/they world reflects our own internal split between the ego on the one hand—which is the belief in separation, fear, punishment, and death—and Spirit on the other, which is the knowledge of love and eternal life. We project this division onto the physical world by always seeing the enemy as "out there" rather than within ourselves.

Although all belief systems quickly become resistant to change, the ego is no ordinary belief system in this regard. It is extremely resistant. It holds incredible power in our unconscious mind and carries an enormous bloc of votes when it comes to making decisions about who we think we are. This belief system is so very powerful that it appears to be an entity in its own right—and we have named it the ego.

We have become trapped in the belief in separation to such a degree that it has become our reality. We have been living the myth of separation for eons, making real the idea that we chose separation by naming it Original Sin. In actuality, no separation ever occurred. We are as much a part of God as we always were. We are spiritual beings having a human experience, remember? Consequently, there is no such thing as Original Sin in this sense.

Jesus purportedly gave us this revelation—the truth about our illusion—in *A Course in Miracles*, a three-volume work by Jesus channeled through a lady named Helen Schucman, the purpose of which was to show us the error of the ego's way and to teach us that the way home to God is through forgiveness. (Interestingly, Helen was a very reluctant channel and never believed a word of what she channeled.) Contrary to some prevailing Christian theology, many biblical scholars find these very same ideas expressed in the Bible.

Anyway, contrary to what the ego would have us believe, the truth is that we actually come to the physical plane with God's blessing and His unconditional love. God always will honor our free will and our choices at the highest level and will offer no divine intervention—unless asked.

Fortunately, Radical Forgiveness provides the perfect tool for asking for such assistance because, in the process, you demonstrate to God that you have seen beyond the ego and glimpsed the truth that only love is real and that we are all one with God, including those who seemed at first to be our enemy.

## 2. THE EGO AS LOVING GUIDE

This other, friendlier way of looking at the ego—which I find equally tenable and, to be truthful, more attractive—holds that, far from being our enemy, the ego is a part of our soul that acts as our guide in the World of Humanity. Its role is to provide opportunities in our lifetime that will fully test our ability to fulfill the mission we carefully planned before we incarnated, the primary purpose of which was to experience a certain agreed-upon amount of separation. When we have reached the degree of separation we signed up for, the process of awakening can begin. That's when we are likely to find Radical Forgiveness.

(By the way, I am certain in my own mind that simply by virtue of your having picked up this book and gotten this far into it without throwing it at the wall, you have arrived at the awakening point or are some distance beyond it. This doesn't mean that you are fully awake all the time—very few people are—but that you are at least beginning to see what's real and remembering the truth.)

(For a full and detailed explanation of this whole idea of our volunteering to experience the pain of separation—and then, when we have reached the amount we contracted to have, beginning the awakening process—see my book *Getting to Heaven on a Harley*.)

The only value in having the human experience is precisely to live through such things as the ego provides: belief in duality, separateness, pain and suffering, guilt and fear. Our ego gives us the opportunity

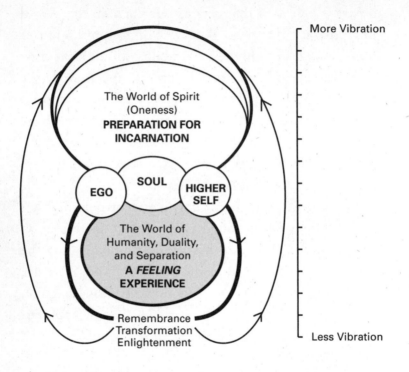

FIGURE 6   **The Soul's Journey**

to embody these feelings by creating experiences like abandonment, betrayal, abuse, rejection, divorce, physical illness, disability, and so on.

Our ego, then, in this model, is the guide that will take us on all these exciting journeys into separation, pain, and discomfort. It does so not out of malice or for the sake of its own survival, as many spiritual teachers maintain, but because it loves us and knows that we need these experiences for our spiritual growth.

The Higher Self is our other guide, who waits patiently while we journey into illusion with the ego until we are ready to awaken. It is through the gentle whispers of the Higher Self that we wake up, bit by bit, until we finally remember who we are. It is often at this point in our lives that we shift our direction and focus less on material things and become more interested in being of service.

I invite you to consider both definitions to be true at the same time. My sense is that the first one is true in terms of explaining our initial descent into physical form and how we came to see that event (falsely) in retrospect, but that the second is grounded in a deeper truth—namely, that we need the ego to help us to fulfill our mission.

Maybe they are two different things; I don't know. It really doesn't matter. Each definition helps me to make sense of this human experience in terms of spiritual truth, and I trust they will do the same for you.

# 7  Hideouts and Scapegoats

UNDERSTANDING THE ROLE the twin psychological ego-defense mechanisms of repression and projection play in how we heal relationships is essential to the concept of Radical Forgiveness. A closer inspection of the mechanisms of each might be helpful.

Operating together, repression and projection wreak havoc upon our relationships and our lives. Together they create and maintain the victim archetype. Understanding how they work enables us to counteract the ego's use of them to keep us separated from each other and from God.

## REPRESSION

Operating as a normal psychological defense mechanism, repression occurs when feelings like terror, guilt, or rage become so overwhelming that the mind simply blocks them entirely from conscious awareness. This makes repression a powerful mental safety device, for without this blocking mechanism we could easily go mad. It works so effectively that absolutely no memory of the feelings, or the event which precipitated them, remains. It can be completely blocked from conscious awareness for days, weeks, or years—sometimes even for the rest of the lifetime.

## Suppression

Repression should not be confused with this other similar but less severe defense mechanism. Suppression occurs when we *consciously* refuse to acknowledge emotions we do not want to feel or express. Though we know they are there, we try to push, or stuff, them away and refuse to deal with them. But their continued denial for long periods of time may lead to a numbness equivalent to their becoming repressed.

## Repressed Guilt and Shame

Guilt and shame are not the same. We feel guilt when we feel we have *done* wrong. Shame takes us to a much deeper level of guilt where we have a sense of actually *being* wrong. With shame, the ego makes us feel inherently wrong at the very core of our being—a feeling that most reliably separates us from everyone and everything. Such shame can be so strong that we have no choice but to repress it: we absolutely could not handle it otherwise.

## Shame Blocks Energy

Young children can be easily shamed, say, when they wet themselves, get an erection, show anger, act shy, and so on. While these may be natural occurrences, the children nevertheless feel shame, and the cumulative effects of this feeling can become overwhelming. Consequently, they repress their shame, but it remains in the unconscious mind as well as in the body. It becomes locked into their system at the cellular level and creates an energy block in the body. If left unresolved for too long, this block gives rise to either mental/emotional problems, physical problems, or both. Repressed emotion is now recognized by many researchers to be one of the principal causes of cancer.

## Repressed Feelings

A large trauma, such as the death of a parent, can cause a child to repress emotion. Likewise, something as seemingly insignificant as a casual critical remark interpreted as meaningful, or an event incorrectly assumed to be the child's fault, can cause emotions to be repressed. For example, children nearly always interpret a divorce as their fault. Research suggests that children remember conversations their parents had while they were still in the womb, so a discussion about an unwanted pregnancy before birth can lead to a child's feeling unwanted and afraid of being abandoned. Such feelings would be repressed even at such an early time in the child's life.

## Generational Guilt

Groups and even nationalities commonly repress accumulated generational guilt. Without doubt, this is the case now with black and white Americans over slavery. The racial problems we now experience in America all stem from the unresolved and repressed guilt within white people and unresolved and repressed rage in blacks.

It has become clear to me during my workshops that a lot of the pain people carry is not their own and may go back several generations. Most frequently it is their parents' pain they have taken on, but it might also be their grandparents' or siblings'. When we are children, our energy is purer and less fractured than it is when we become adults, so children feel able to carry that pain where a wounded adult may not. But children forget to give it back, and they make it their own.

## The Dark Side

We also experience intense shame over aspects of ourselves we dislike and, therefore, disown. Carl Jung, the famous Swiss psychoanalyst, referred to this as our shadow because it represents the dark side of ourselves, the part we do not want to see or have seen by others. This part of ourselves knows we are capable of killing another human being—knows we could have taken part in the concentration camps had we been German during that time, knows we might have owned and brutalized slaves had we been born white in the South before the Civil War, could hurt or rape someone, is greedy or avaricious, is rageful and vengeful, or is in some other way deviant or unacceptable. Any such characteristics we possess or areas of our lives that bring us feelings of shame we classify as our shadow and repress.

### Sitting on a Volcano

Repressing this kind of energy is like sitting on a volcano! We never know when our strength will give out, thus allowing the lava (shadow) to spurt forth and wreak havoc on our world. This explains why we need to bring in a scapegoat on whom we can project all that shame. That way, we can be free of it, at least temporarily.

## PROJECTION

Even when we have repressed the feelings and/or memories associated with a life event, we know on an unconscious level that the shame, guilt, or self-criticism associated with it remains with us. So we attempt to rid ourselves of that pain by "taking it out of ourselves" and transferring it onto someone or something else outside of ourselves. This projection process allows us to forget we ever possessed such feelings.

Once we project what we do not want to own onto someone else, we see them, rather than ourselves, as possessing those qualities. So if we repress our guilt and then project it, we make the other person the wrong one. If we repress our anger and then project it, we see them as the one who's angry. We can accuse them of all the things we feared we would be accused of ourselves. No wonder we feel so relieved when we project! In so doing, we make someone else responsible for everything terrible that happens to us and for what we see as negative about ourselves. Then we can demand that they be punished, so we can feel even more righteous and safe from attack.

This explains why we love to watch the news on television. The news provides us with an opportunity to project all our guilt and shame onto the murderers, rapists, corrupt politicians, and other "bad" people we see on the screen. After doing so, we can go to bed feeling okay about ourselves. The news, and all the other television programs that feature "bad" people and situations, endlessly provides us with convenient scapegoats upon whom to project.

Projecting
self-righteous
indignation, anger,
and judgment

You disgust me!
You are such a liar
and a cheat!

FIGURE 7 **Projecting Our Repressed Shame**

*Recognize When You're Projecting*
As soon as you find yourself judging someone and getting
angry, you know you are projecting. Anger serves as the
constant companion of projection, for you always use
this emotion to justify the projection of your self-hatred.

What you find so objectionable about this person
simply serves as a reflection of that part of you that
you have rejected and denied in yourself (your shadow)
and projected onto them instead. If this were not so,
you would not be upset.

*If You Spot It, You Got It!*
It feels like the other person is doing something to you
to make you angry. However, when you own that your

feelings begin with you, not with them, you will drop the need to feel victimized and realize that the person is doing these things not *to* you but *for* you—enabling you to take back the projection and love it in yourself.

Though repression and projection are meant as temporary relief valves for the psyche, the ego coopts them as the means to increase and prolong the feeling of separation. Hence, denial, repression, and projection become permanent ways of being for us, at least until we begin to awaken. At that point we slowly become aware of these mechanisms and how we use them to create and maintain separation. The task then is to wean ourselves off these mechanisms and begin to take responsibility for creating the circumstances of our lives rather than blaming everything on others.

### Fear of Intimacy ("Into-Me-See")

Every person we meet offers us the opportunity to choose between projection or forgiveness, union or separation. However, when it comes to close personal relationships, the more intimate we become with someone the closer they get to our true self. Thus it becomes all the more likely they will discover all that unpleasant stuff (our shadow material) that we have denied and repressed, the prospect of which creates enormous fear inside us. The temptation to project it all onto them becomes almost irresistible. At this point, the honeymoon is over. The fear of intimacy becomes so strong that the relationship is likely to fall apart. Most do so within six months to a year, often with a lot of acrimony and painful emotion.

## ALL RELATIONSHIPS ARE FOR HEALING

To be awake means to fully understand how this all works and how the ego has skillfully used our spiritual intelligence—which is always moving us in the direction of healing and growing—to provide us with people whose role it is to mirror our own projections and repressed self-hatred. Only then can we heal the separation within ourselves and become whole. This is the purpose of all relationships.

As we saw in Jill's story, Radical Forgiveness can save a relationship (Jill and Jeff are still happily married). However, this is not necessarily the goal. If the true purpose of the relationship has been fulfilled, which is to say the healing has occurred, the relationship may simply dissolve naturally and peacefully. When both parties understand Radical Forgiveness and use the technology, the parting can be loving, respectful, and relatively pain free.

If, on the other hand, the relationship breaks off before the healing has taken place, the parties will likely go off and find another partner with very similar characteristics who will resonate the same issues for them all over again. Many of us do this over and over again, and we can often see the pattern quite clearly when it is pointed out.

# 8 Attraction and Resonance

As WE SAW in the previous chapter, we project our guilt and anger onto people who have the capacity to resonate with our feelings, and such people become convenient scapegoats.

Just as a radio station uses a certain frequency to broadcast its programs, so our emotions (energy in motion) vibrate at certain frequencies. People who resonate with our feelings vibrate at that same rate and are likely to have a similar emotion pattern to our own—either the same or the opposite—which they then mirror back to us.

Our core beliefs also have a certain frequency. By speaking them aloud, we give our beliefs even more energy, and they take on a causal quality in the Universe, causing effects in our world. In addition, other people resonate with the energetic frequency of that belief. In other words, they vibrate sympathetically at the same rate with it. When they do so, they are attracted into our lives to mirror our beliefs back to us. This gives us a chance to look at and, if necessary, change our minds about that belief. It is not only negative beliefs that get mirrored back to us. For example, if we are loving and trusting, we will tend to attract people into our lives who are likewise trustworthy and nurturing.

Recall from Part One that my sister, Jill, had a belief that she would never be enough for any man. This belief resonated with a man who was a sex addict. He provided the ideal partner for her because he supported her belief by continually having sex with other women, thus showing her she was not enough for him. She did not make the connection in that relationship and, consequently, did not heal the pain that created this belief in the first place. So she found another man (Jeff) who resonated with her belief. He supported her belief differently, by using his own issue of codependence with his daughter Lorraine as the catalyst. In this situation, she saw the connection and realized that he was mirroring her belief that she was not enough, and both of them healed.

If you want to know what you dislike about yourself and have likely disowned, simply look at what annoys you about the people who come into your life. Look into the mirror they provide. If you seem to attract a lot of angry people into your life, you probably have not dealt with some anger of your own. If people seem to withhold love from you, some part of you is unwilling to give love. If people seem to steal things from you, part of you behaves dishonestly or feels dishonest. If people betray you, maybe you have betrayed someone in the past.

Look at the issues that upset you too. If abortion really makes you mad, maybe a part of you shows little reverence for life in other ways, or a part of you knows it could abuse a child. If you are passionately against homosexuality, maybe you cannot accept the part of you that sometimes feels homosexually inclined.

## Hall of Mirrors

The reflection does not always appear so readily or as simply. For example, sometimes we do not identify with the specific behavior as much as we do with the underlying meaning it holds for us. A man who gets angry about his wife's overeating and obesity may not be resonating with any personal tendency to overeat; instead, he might be resonating with her use of food to avoid dealing with emotional problems because it mirrors his tendency to run away from his own emotional turmoil. Clearly, seeing what others mirror for us can become like looking at the myriad of distorted images in a hall of mirrors.

## Automatic Reversal of Projection

The beauty of Radical Forgiveness lies in the fact that it does not require us to recognize what we project. We simply forgive the person for what is happening at the time. In doing so, we automatically undo the projection, no matter how complicated the situation. The reason for this is simple, in that the person represents the original pain that caused us to project in the first place. As we forgive him or her, we clear that original pain.

Ironically, the people who seem to upset us the most are those who, at the soul level, love and support us the most. They are often the souls we made contracts with prior to our incarnation to do certain things with us during our lifetime. Almost always, and often at great expense to themselves in terms of their own discomfort, these individuals try to teach us something about ourselves and encourage us to move toward our awakening. Remember, this is not a personality-to-personality exchange. In fact, more than likely, our personalities clash terribly. Instead, the souls of each player set up the scenario in the hope that we will eventually see the truth.

## Don't Take Life So Personally

Who comes into our lives to help us accomplish this task is actually irrelevant. If one particular person does not take the job, somebody else will. The tragedy is that, as the victim, we seldom understand this. We imagine that we just happened to be the unlucky recipient of a particular person's harmful behavior. It does not occur to us that we might have (at the soul level) attracted the person and the situation to ourselves for a reason and that had it not been this person, it simply would have been someone else. We mistakenly feel that, but for this person, we would not have had the problem. In other words, we see the problem as entirely with the other person, whom we now feel justified in hating and resenting for "causing" us pain and unhappiness.

### Blaming Our Parents

We often hear this type of blame when people talk about their parents. "If I'd had different parents, I'd be whole and complete today," people say. Wrong. They could have chosen a different set of parents, that's true; but the new set would have given them the exact same experience, because that's what their soul wanted.

### Repeating Relationship Patterns

When we see ourselves as victims, we think only about killing the messenger. We miss the message. This explains why people go from marriage to marriage recreating the same relationship dynamic each time. They do not get the message with the first spouse, so they go on to another who continues trying to relay the message the last spouse tried to relay.

## Codependency and Mutual Projection

We also find others onto whom we project our own self-hatred, who will not only accept it but recipro-cate by projecting theirs back onto us. We call this kind of agreement a codependent or addictive relation-ship. This special someone compensates for what we feel is missing in ourselves by continually telling us we are okay, so we avoid feeling our shame about who we are. We do the same thing for them in return; thus both people learn to manipulate each other with highly conditional love based on the underlying guilt. (The stereotypical Jewish mother is a wonderful example of this archetype.) The moment the other person with-draws approval, we are forced to confront our guilt and self-hatred again, and everything collapses. Love turns immediately into hate, and each partner attacks the other. This explains why so many faltering rela-tionships that once seemed supportive and loving turn into cauldrons of hate almost instantaneously.

# 9 Cause and Effect

CENTRAL TO THE idea that we create our own reality is the Law of Cause and Effect. This states that every action has an equal reaction. Therefore, every cause must have an effect, and every effect must have a cause. Since thoughts are causal in nature, every thought has an effect in the world. In other words, we—unconsciously for the most part—create our world, the World of Humanity, with our thoughts.

When we vibrate at a high frequency, such as when we pray, meditate, or contemplate, we can create consciously and intentionally through thought. Most of the time, though, we do so quite unconsciously. Individual random thoughts do not carry a lot of energy, so they create a relatively small effect. However, thoughts accompanied by larger amounts of energy, especially emotional or creative energy, have a much larger effect in the world. Thus they take a larger hand in creating our reality.

When a thought gathers sufficient energy to become a belief, it has an even greater effect in the world. It becomes an operating principle in our lives, and we then create effects—circumstances, situations, even physical events—that hold true to that belief. What we believe about the world is how it will always be for us.

Acceptance of the principle that thought is creative is fundamental to an understanding of Radical Forgiveness, for it allows us to see that what turns up in our lives represents what we have created with our thoughts and beliefs. It allows us to see that we are simply projecting all our thoughts and beliefs about "the way things are" onto the world.

FIGURE 8   **Projecting Our Own Reality**

## PROJECTING THE ILLUSION

Metaphorically, we run a movie called Reality through our minds (the projector), and we project it "out there." Once we understand that what we call reality is just our projections, instead of blaming others we can begin to take responsibility for what we have created with our thoughts. When we change our perception and drop our attachment to our belief that what appears on the screen represents reality, we experience Radical Forgiveness.

*Consciousness Determines What Happens*
While it may seem difficult to see the principle of cause and effect operating in our lives, it becomes apparent when we trace back from what is occurring. In other words, if you want to know your beliefs, just look at what is happening; that will tell you what you are projecting. For example, if you keep getting attacked or disasters keep happening to you, the likelihood is that you believe the world is inherently an unsafe place. You are creating these events to prove that you are right about that and people are supporting you in this belief by appearing to you to behave in a threatening or dangerous manner.

Some friends of mine have a spiritual conference center in the mountains of North Carolina. Werner, being of a prudent nature, thought he and his wife, Jean, should have insurance to protect their buildings against fire, storm damage, and the frequent tornadoes that come through each season. Jean was very much against the idea. She felt having such insurance would clearly indicate to the Universe that they did not trust in their safety. Now, I am not advocating this, but they decided against purchasing the insurance.

The following year, a huge storm hit their very mountain and devastated the area. Thousands of trees were uprooted and thrown down. When my wife and I drove up to visit them two weeks later, we couldn't believe our eyes: it looked like a war zone. They had obviously been obliged to cut their way out. The storm had happened while thirty-six people were at the center attending a conference, and they were unable to leave for two whole days. But in spite of all the trees down, not a single car or any of the buildings were touched—and all were right in among the trees. Trees fell within inches of structures and autos but miraculously damaged nothing. For my friends, it was a great confirmation of their faith and willingness to trust.

Looking at this from a cause-and-effect standpoint, Jean recognized that buying insurance reinforced a belief (a cause) in adversity and would create the energy for something bad (an effect) to happen. Instead she chose the thought (cause) "We are doing God's work here, and we are absolutely safe." The effect, as it played out in the world, was that in the midst of chaos nothing bad happened.

As I have said, if you want to know your beliefs, look at what you have in your life—or what you do not have. If, for example, you do not have love in your life and do not seem to be able to create a loving relationship, examine your beliefs about self-worth, or about safety with the opposite sex. Of course, this may not be as easy as it sounds, for the beliefs you hold may be buried deep in your subconscious mind.

### You Don't Need to Know Why

The good news is that you do not have to know why you created your situation or what beliefs led you to its creation. Just seeing the situation's existence as an opportunity to perceive it differently—*being willing* to see it as perfect—is enough to bring about the required shift in perception and a healing of the original pain.

The truth is, we in the World of Humanity cannot know *why* a situation is as it is because the answer lies in the World of Divine Truth, and we can know little or nothing of that world as long as we are in human form. *All we can do is surrender to the situation.*

## Just Surrender

If new insights or connections, old memories, emotional movements, and other psychic events are necessary for the desired change to occur, they will happen automatically and without our conscious control. If we try to figure it all out and manipulate the unfolding process, this creates resistance and blocks the process completely, which puts us right back under the influence of the ego.

## Freedom from the Law

It is important to realize that the Law of Cause and Effect only applies to the World of Humanity. It is a physical law, not a spiritual law. Creating an open parking space or any other physical thing that you desire and create with your mind is still only manipulating the illusion. It has little to do with being spiritual as such. In fact, if we imagine that we are special because of how well we can manifest in the world, this simply increases our sense of separation and strengthens the ego.

On the other hand, when we truly drop the need to know the why or how of everything, let go of our need to control the world, and truly surrender to what is—as is—in the knowledge that the love of God is in everything, we shall transcend the Law of Cause and Effect entirely. Then we shall realize that karma is just another story that exists only in our minds in the World of Humanity. In the World of Divine Truth, there is no such thing as karma or cause and effect. There is only first cause, which is God.

However, if we engage in activities and consistent ways of being that result in our vibration being significantly raised (through the continual and sustained use of Radical Forgiveness over a long period of time, for instance), we may find ourselves becoming "first cause."

That would be in stark contrast to how it is for the majority of us at the present time, where we are always the "effect" in this cause-and-effect world—always having to react to what appears to be happening "out there."

Perhaps in the not-too-distant future, when our vibratory rate is raised and we have all our energy and consciousness in present time rather than tied up in past or future, we will find ourselves not so much noticing synchronicities as *becoming* synchronicity itself.

For more on how to gauge your own vibratory rate, how you stack up against the "enlightened" ones, and how many it would take of a certain vibration to shift planetary consciousness, I recommend David Hawkins's book *Power vs. Force*, published by Hay House.

# 10  Mission "Forgiveness"

NOT ONE OF us can feel our soul's journey to be over until we, as an entire species, have completed the mission we created for ourselves. This involves no less than transforming the energies of fear, death, and duality by coming to the full realization of our oneness—that we are not separated from God at all and that these energies are simply illusion. This is our collective mission; each of us serves as an individual expression of that mission, and the life we create for ourselves here in the World of Humanity purely serves that purpose. There are no exceptions. Whether we know it or not, we are all on that spiritual path.

## OUR INDIVIDUAL MISSION

The decision about which energies we work with on the earth plane is not made by us at the human level. That decision predates our incarnation and is made by our soul group—a group to which we belong made up of souls who either incarnate with us or act as our spirit guides during our incarnation.

Once it is decided which energies we will work with, we then carefully choose parents who will provide the experiences we need as children, and we arrange for others to come along at the right time to play their respective roles in the experiences necessary to the accomplishment of our mission. We create dramas throughout our physical lives that allow us to experience the feelings that make up our mission. These dramas serve as opportunities to experience the separation we came to experience. Then we can awaken, forgive, and remember who we are.

## MISSION AMNESIA

Seen from the World of Divine Truth prior to incarnation, the mission seems easy. But once we incarnate, it takes on a new level of difficulty. This is due not only to the greater density of energy in the World of Humanity but to the fact that the mission must be undertaken free of any awareness that we have chosen this experience. If we knew (remembered) the truth about our purpose, the experience would be pointless. How can we remember who we are if we have never forgotten? So Spirit creates the human experience in such a way that when we are born into our bodies we lose all recall of our mission and all awareness that life on the physical plane is, in fact, a setup.

To accomplish our mission (to transform energies) we must have a total experience of those energies. For example, to transform the energy of "victim," we must feel utterly victimized. To transform the energy of fear, we must feel terrorized. To transform the energy of hate, we must be consumed with hatred. In other words, we must go fully into the experience of being human. It is only when we have fully felt the emotions connected with these energies that we gain the ability to move into the full forgiveness of them. And it is through forgiving them that we remember who we are.

From this viewpoint, we are clearly never in a position to judge anyone. A person who appears hateful may have chosen as his mission to transform that energy. Thus his hateful behavior, even though it seems to harm others (who may have volunteered to have hate projected at them as their mission), is neither right nor wrong. His hateful behavior simply represents what needs to happen to transform the energy of hate. Period.

The energy of hate is transformed when someone who feels hated sees the love beneath the hate and forgives the person for hating him. In that moment, hearts open and love flows between the two people. Thus hate is transformed into love. Awakening results from a continuous process of transformation of the energies of all forms of separation.

### Janet's Story

Janet, who had cancer, attended one of my early cancer retreats, but her tumor was not the only thing eating away at her. The anger she felt concerning her twenty-three-year-old daughter, Melanie, was doing the same.

By all accounts, Melanie exhibited some pretty strong rebellious behavior. She was verbally abusive to Janet and Janet's new husband, Jim, and she had attached herself to a rather unsavory man. "I hate her with a vengeance," Janet related. "Her behavior toward me and Jim is simply abominable, and I can't stand it anymore. I really hate her."

We dug a little deeper into Janet's personal history and found that a similar relationship had existed between Janet and her own mother. It was not as clear and dramatic as the drama with Melanie, but the dynamic was similar. Janet had resented how much her mother had controlled her and tried to run her life. She did not rebel as Melanie did, though. Instead she had become withdrawn and cold toward her mother.

We began to explore how the dynamic with Melanie reflected her soul's willingness to help Janet heal her issues with her mother, but Janet was not willing to see this. She was simply too angry to hear anything that did not correspond with her feelings. So we asked her to move into her anger, to feel and express it by beating cushions with a tennis racket and shouting. (Anger is very effectively released through the combination of physical action and the use of the voice.) Although she released some anger toward her mother, her anger with Melanie remained.

### Janet's Satori

That evening's retreat session was reserved for Satori Breath. To experience Satori Breath and use it for healing, everyone in the group lies on the floor and breathes consciously and vigorously for about an hour while listening to loud music. (See Chapter 27.) While this may sound bizarre, breathing in this manner often results in emotional release, insight, and integration of change at the cellular level. That night, Janet had her *satori*—her "awakening."

After the breathing session, people began sharing what had happened for them during the exercise. As soon as Janet began to share, we knew something important had happened. Her voice was soft and sweet, whereas before it had been hard and abrasive. Her posture was relaxed and open, whereas before it had been tight and constricted. There was not a trace of the anger that had filled her being and that we all had felt emanating from her previously. She was calm and evidently peaceful. In fact, she hardly seemed the same person. "I have no idea what all this means," she began. "All I know is that I saw something while I was breathing, and it felt more real than anything I can possibly describe. Nothing much happened for quite a while after I began breathing," she continued. "Then, suddenly, I found myself floating in space, out there in the ethers. I was not in a body, and I knew with certainty that I was re-experiencing a time before I came into my current life. I was pure spirit. I have never felt so peaceful and calm. Then I became aware of Melanie, also in spirit form. She came close, and we began to dance together—just dancing in space without limitation.

"We began a conversation about coming into our next lifetime together," Janet said. "This lifetime. The big question we had to decide was who would play what role—who was going to play the mother and who was going to play the daughter. It didn't much matter, for either way it was going to be a difficult assignment for us both. It would be a very strong test of our love. We had to decide, so we agreed that I would be the mother and she would be the daughter and that we would incarnate soon thereafter. That's about it," she concluded. "It doesn't sound like a whole lot happened, but really it did. I just can't put it into words. I just can't describe the depth and the meaning of what I experienced."

*Energies Transformed*

We discussed her experience and looked at the notion of mission as suggested by Janet's vision. Several others in the group felt strongly about her experience and saw parallels in their own lives. I suggested that Janet say nothing at all to Melanie when she returned home after the retreat. Within a few days of Janet's homecoming, Melanie called her mother and asked if she could come and talk. Janet agreed, and, while the first meeting was tentative and awkward, their relationship changed dramatically after that. Melanie soon dropped all her bizarre behavior, sent the unsavory boyfriend packing, and came home to be with her mother and take care of her during her illness. They literally became best friends and were quite inseparable after that. Also, Janet's mother began calling more often, and gradually their relationship began to improve as well.

In this example, the transformation of energy happened in a roundabout way. Janet was extremely resistant to forgiving Melanie. Her soul guided her to the retreat so that she could do a process that opened her to a remembrance of her mission agreement, which in turn enabled her to see the perfection in the situation. By forgiving Melanie, she transformed the hate in their relationship and, as a result, healed the original pain between herself and her mother.

## MISSIONS TO HEAL THE COLLECTIVE

While all of us come in to heal aspects of our own soul or those of our soul group, some may incarnate with a larger role to play. This may be to take on particular energies that get played out at the social, political, national, and international level and offer large groups of people the opportunity to heal.

Of course, as with all missions, it may not look anything like a healing opportunity. It may show up as war or famine or maybe a natural disaster. But when we open to the possibility that a group soul healing is being offered and that the whole thing is being orchestrated by Spirit for the greater good of all souls involved, we begin to see things very differently. Let me give you some seemingly outrageous examples.

1. Suppose the soul who came in to become Adolf Hitler did so with a mission to transform the victim consciousness of the Jewish race and the superiority consciousness of the German race.

2. What if Saddam Hussein came in to help American consciousness transform its guilt about slavery and the terrible abuse of its own people? (See my book *A Radical Incarnation,* which explores this possibility.)

3. Suppose Slobodan Milošević came in to enable America to project onto him the self-hatred it feels about the ethnic cleansing it has perpetrated against the Native American people.

4. What if the Chinese government had to invade Tibet so the Dalai Lama would be forced to travel the world and spread his beautiful message beyond the borders of his country?

5. Suppose the soul that was Princess Diana chose to die in exactly the way she did, and when she did, in order to open the heart chakra of England.

In the first edition of this book Princess Diana's story appeared as the Epilogue. That was because she died within a very few days of my going to press, so it had to go in almost as an afterthought. In this new edition, I am including it in this chapter since it is so pertinent to the issue of mission.

129

The event was still very fresh in my mind when I first wrote about Diana's death. The funeral had only just taken place and the emotional outpouring was still continuing. I was still very much in the experience of it all, and I think that comes across in the piece. For that reason, I have decided not to alter the original version in any way so that you may experience the satori vicariously through my own experience of it.

### Good-bye England's Rose

I began this book with a story about my sister, Jill. Its purpose was to illustrate how a seemingly desperate situation can be transformed when we approach it from the standpoint of Radical Forgiveness.

Just a few days before going to press, fate handed me an opportunity to end the book with a story that was equally instructive and open to a Radical Forgiveness perspective. Unlike the one about Jill, this story was one with which virtually everyone in the world was familiar, as well as deeply involved emotionally. I refer of course to the story of Princess Diana, who made her unexpected transition in the early hours of Sunday, August 31, 1997.

The drama began for me when my lifetime friend Peter Jollyman woke me with a phone call from England. For him it was around midday, but for me, in

Atlanta, it was still early and I had not yet seen a newspaper or listened to the radio.

"Have you heard about the accident?" he asked.

"What accident?" I replied, still in a stupor but aware enough to realize this had to be serious for him to be calling.

"Princess Di was killed last night in a car crash in Paris. She was being chased by paparazzi. Her car spun out of control and hit a concrete post. She and Dodi were killed."

I noticed a perfunctory pang of remorse pass through me as I listened to the details as best he knew them at the time, but I can't say that it lasted more than a few moments. I tried to sound suitably shocked, but I really felt somewhat ambivalent about it.

Lots of people died in the last twenty-four hours, I thought after I put the phone down. Why would her death be any more, or any less, tragic than anyone else's? It was her time to go, and that's about all there is to it. Sad for her two boys though, of course. With that, I went downstairs to make tea and fix breakfast.

Then I turned on the TV and, from that moment on, was gradually drawn into and involved with what was to become, in the days culminating in her funeral on Saturday morning, a roller coaster of emotion.

As the days went by, I realized that something quite extraordinary was going on. The reaction to Princess Diana's death, not only in England but throughout the world, was truly phenomenal. As I saw my countrymen on the TV in heartfelt pain, crying and grieving in public—something English people simply do not do ordinarily—I found myself feeling the same emotions and crying with them. I was shocked to realize that I was hurting too. Somehow this woman, whom I had never met or thought much about, especially during the thirteen years I had lived in the U.S., had touched me deeply. I felt the loss profoundly, and I was very surprised.

I began to pay attention and to wonder what was really happening here. Something of extraordinarily deep significance was occurring, and I began an inner search to find the message and the meaning in it. Diana's death clearly had meaning far beyond the apparent circumstances in which it occurred, dramatic as they appeared to be. Some higher purpose was being played out here, I thought.

Then, on Wednesday, it hit me. As I watched the scenes from England and experienced the great outpouring of emotion from people not in the least renowned for showing their emotions, especially in the open, I suddenly realized what Diana's spiritual mission had been. The overarching purpose of her incarnation had been to open the heart chakra of Great Britain and, by so doing, greatly accelerate the spiritual evolution of the British people, no less. I had no doubt whatsoever that she had achieved exactly that.

No one who watched the events of that week could ever doubt that she had single-handedly transformed the country—and indeed, much of the world—at the heart level. Only a very few people in all of human history come to mind as having had such an effect on the world purely through the expression of love energy: Gandhi, Martin Luther King Jr., and Nelson Mandela perhaps; Mother Teresa and Jesus Christ, certainly. (No wonder the Queen of England bowed her head to Diana's coffin—something never before witnessed.)

While in terms of human achievement and spiritual example in life, any comparison with Mother Teresa would be unfair. It is nevertheless interesting to note that the death of Mother Teresa, whose life and work, in most people's eyes, brought her close to sainthood in her lifetime, did not take the spotlight off Diana for even a moment. That two women whose lives so deeply touched the world through authentic love should make their transitions within days of each other has enormous spiritual significance.

Even though the British people had been through two wars this century, suffering and grieving enormous losses, they had come through it all with their legendary sense of humor and proverbial stiff upper lip intact —but not, I think it is fair to say, with an open heart. That had to wait, not only for the coming of a people's princess but for her divinely planned and, to us at least, untimely and tragic death.

Since then, commentators have tried in vain to explain her effect on the world in terms of our fixation on, and willingness to almost deify, celebrities we know only through the media. Jonathan Alter, in *Newsweek*, came closer than most by referring to what Richard Sennett, in *The Fall of Public Man*, called the ideology of intimacy, in which people "seek to find personal meaning in impersonal situations." It is true that people did not know her personally, and to that extent it remains an impersonal situation. Yet she transcended those limitations imposed by time and space and somehow touched everyone's heart very deeply in a way that cannot be easily explained.

The key to understanding her power as a human being lies in the archetype of the wounded healer, which teaches us that our power lies in our wounds—in the sense that it is the wound in me that evokes the healing in you and the wound in you that evokes the healing in me. We are all wounded healers, but we don't know it. When we keep our wounds hidden and totally private, we separate from and deny healing, not only to ourselves but to countless others. The stiff upper lip is a terrible way to withhold love. It atrophies the heart and cripples the soul. Through her willingness to share her deepest wounds with the whole world, Princess Diana evoked the healer in all of us, opened our hearts, and healed our fractured souls.

The whole world watched as people took their cue from Diana and opened up, sharing their grief and their woundedness, just as she had done. She gave the people a language of intimacy they could use to express feelings openly and authentically. I don't recall seeing one display of emotion and feeling that was not truly authentic; and on television today, that is indeed unusual.

As we each begin to emerge from behind the pain of loss and the rope burns of grief, anger, and projection of guilt regarding our insatiable appetite for Diana's image and curiosity about her life—which the press and paparazzi merely reflected for us—we begin to discern, through the mists and veils, the divine perfection of it all. The more we contemplate the mission she accepted and the extent to which she succeeded, the more we are able to surrender into that perfection.

We find ourselves experiencing a new level of peace as we move beyond the emotions and thoughts that once would have tied us to the World of Humanity forever and held us hostage to the victim archetype; we move toward accepting the fact that it all had to unfold in exactly that way. The mission absolutely required the upbringing she had, the marriage that went terribly wrong, the rejection she suffered at the hands of the royal establishment, the criticism by the press, the hounding by the paparazzi, the dramatic and violent death—everything, down to the very last detail.

As the future unfolds, you will notice that now that Diana has returned "home," having completed her mission, the energies that held all those dynamics in place will begin to disperse. Not only is she released from those dynamics, so are all the other people who were involved in the drama we know to be only an illusion. Charles is now free to become warmer, less distant, and a more loving father to his two boys—and he undoubtedly will. (The press will say that he changed because of what happened, but we will know the real truth.) The Queen will probably become less stuffy, more open, and not quite so irrelevant. The monarchy itself will transcend the cult of personality and will become a stronger, more meaningful institution, not as a direct response to what happened but because of the energy shift that occurred when the mission was over and the transformation complete.

But just because someone opens his or her heart chakra, there's no guarantee that he or she will keep it open. That remains a matter of choice at every moment. The same is true of the collective. The British people, and others around the world, will either stay in the love vibration that Diana's death catapulted them into, and use that power to transform themselves, their royal family, and their society, or they will focus on the illusion of what happened, blaming Charles, the royal family in general, the driver, the press, and others. If they choose the latter, that will be their choice and perfect in its own way, but it will cause the collective heart chakra to close again.

Perhaps this book has a part to play in keeping the collective heart chakra open. Maybe the insight you have gained by reading it will enable you to remain focused not on the illusion of what happened in the tunnel that night in Paris but on what is real in the Princess Diana story, from beginning to end, and the mission that gave it meaning and significance.

Maybe everyone who reads this book will truly recognize and acknowledge that, just as Jeff played his part for Jill in the story in Part One, Charles played his part beautifully for Diana—as did Camilla Parker-Bowles and the Queen. Maybe it will be clear to everyone who reads this book that the drama called for such loving, courageous souls to play those parts in exactly those ways and, let it be said, at great cost to themselves. (Charles's sacrifice for the sake of the opening of the heart chakra of Britain was absolutely no less than Diana's—in fact, in ordinary human terms, it was probably greater. It may have cost him his crown, no less!)

Maybe, too, it will be obvious to everyone that it was all agreed upon in advance, prior to each character's soul incarnating into this world, and that the paparazzi also played an essential and loving part in all this, as did the editors who paid for intrusive pictures of Diana.

Those who are indeed able to do the Radical Forgiveness reframe to this extent, recognizing that there were no victims here, will be a great beacon of light to all those who might otherwise choose to focus on the illusion, close their hearts, and lose the love vibration. It is my fervent hope that every reader who is changed by my book will become a beacon of love— taking over where Diana left off, helping people to stay in this new and higher vibration that her perfectly timed transition triggered.

# 11 Transforming
## the Victim Archetype

As WE SAW in the last chapter, our primary mission is to transform the victim archetype and raise the consciousness of the planet. But what does it mean to transform anything, and how does it raise consciousness?

The first thing to understand is that we can transform something only when we choose doing so as our spiritual mission. And we make the decision about our mission not in this world but in the World of Divine Truth prior to incarnating.

The second thing to realize is that transforming something *does not* mean changing it. In fact:

To transform anything we must experience it
fully and love it just the way it is.

For example, maybe your individual mission involved being born into an abusive family to experience the abuse firsthand and to know it either as a victim or as a perpetrator. Remember, once you incarnate, your memory of your agreed-upon mission disappears. If you recalled your mission, you would not experience the energy and the feelings of victimhood as fully. Only in the experience of being victimized can you possibly come to realize what lies behind the illusion of victimhood—the projection of your self-hatred. If you are able to look beyond the illusion of the perpetrator and recognize these actions as a call for love, and if you respond with love and complete acceptance, the victim energy is transformed and the consciousness of all involved is raised. In addition, the energy that holds the pattern of abuse disappears and the behavior stops immediately. That is what transformation is all about.

On the other hand, if we do not recognize the truth in the situation or do not see beyond the illusion, and if we try to change the physical circumstances, we lock up the energy that holds the pattern of abuse in place and nothing changes. What you resist persists.

## ONLY LOVE TRANSFORMS

Only love has the ability to transform energies like child abuse, corporate greed, murder, and all the other so-called evils of the world. Nothing else has any impact. Actions taken to change such situations—such as removing a child from an abusive environment—while humane in and of themselves, do not create transformation. The reason for this is simple. First, such action arises from fear, not love. Second, our intervention and judgments maintain the energy patterns of abuse and lock them up more securely.

This explains why the decision to transform something can be made only from the World of Divine Truth. We humans are so locked into our beliefs about pain and suffering, fear and death, that even while we may believe that a particular child's soul came into this world to experience abuse and actually wants to feel abused, we simply cannot stand by and watch this happen. While the mission looks easy from the World of Divine Truth, it appears quite different down here on the physical plane. Who could possibly leave a child in an abusive environment? We cannot help but intervene. We are human!

As we saw in an earlier chapter, we need to surrender to the idea that Spirit knows exactly what it is doing. If it were not in the child's highest and best interest for there to be an intervention on its behalf, Spirit would set things up so that no one notices the abuse. If on the other hand, Spirit decides an intervention serves the soul's highest good, it will arrange for that to occur. But this is not our decision. We as human beings must always respond in the way that seems most humane, most caring and compassionate, while at the same time knowing that love is contained in the situation.

### Radical Forgiveness Transforms

This is not to say that we as humans cannot contribute to the transformation of such energies as those that create child abuse. We do so when we apply Radical Forgiveness to the situation. If we truly forgive—in the radical sense—all those involved in the abusive situation, we definitely have an impact on the energy pattern. Ultimately, the child will have to forgive in order to change the pattern, but each time any of us, in any situation, whether we are personally involved or not, chooses to see the perfection in the situation, we change the energy at once.

I was once asked to address the National Society of Mediators at their annual conference. I was only to have about forty-five minutes and they were to be eating lunch while I spoke! I went early to listen in on their discussions and try to get a feel for their way of thinking. I determined that, in terms of background, about 50 percent of the attendees were lawyers and 50 percent were counselors and that their commitment to mediation left them fairly open-minded and flexible in their approaches to problem-solving.

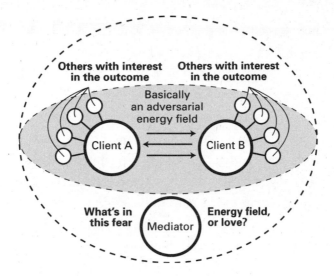

FIGURE 9   **Mediation Energy Fields**

For the first twenty minutes or so, I did my best to explain the concepts and assumptions underlying Radical Forgiveness. Then I drew the diagram above to represent the energetic relationship between them and their clients.

I then put it to them that their perception of the situation they were mediating was likely to be such that what was happening to Clients A and B was unfortunate at best and tragic at worst. I also suggested that they saw their role as mediators as trying to make the best of a bad job and resolve the situation in a way that would be the least damaging to both parties and their dependents.

They agreed that this was a fair characterization of their task and that the energy field around the situation for the clients was one of hostility and mistrust. Had it been otherwise, they wouldn't have needed a mediator.

Then I factored into the situation their own energy. They saw that their energy field would normally contain thoughts and feelings related to the perception that this was a "bad" situation. I also suggested that, even though they were trying to mediate and help both clients, their perception of the situation as "bad" fed into the clients' energy field and reinforced their victim consciousness.

"What if," I asked then, "instead of seeing this situation as tragic and undesirable, you became willing to entertain the idea that this is a divine plan unfolding exactly as it needs to unfold, and that each of the parties, including the ones on the periphery, are in actuality getting exactly what they subconsciously want at the soul level—and that this is true no matter how this situation works out?

"Do you think that would make a difference? Your energy field, instead of being filled with fear-based thoughts and emotions, would be filled with love. Do you think that would have an effect on how the situation would finally become resolved?"

Surprisingly, they understood. Even the lawyers got it! There was broad acceptance of the idea that the way they held the situation in their own minds was a powerful factor in determining how the situation came out. They saw it from a cause-and-effect standpoint. It was not that anything would be done differently or overtly changed; it would just be that by their holding the idea that everything was perfect, the energy would be allowed to move—without as much resistance—in whatever direction it needed to move. That is what transforming energy means.

## MORPHIC RESONANCE

What I have just described draws on Rupert Sheldrake's theory of morphic fields and morphic resonance. Sheldrake is an English biologist who postulates the existence of fields which are self-organizing and self-regulating systems in nature that organize and sustain patterns of vibratory or rhythmic activity. Elements are attracted to each other by morphic resonance to create these fields, which are constantly changing and evolving. When one element in the field changes, this affects the whole field. The concept seems to be applicable at all levels, from quantum phenomena to social group behavior.

In the human context, morphic fields link individual members through extrasensory and energetic resonance (consciousness), a process that is independent of time and space. This is why when someone forgives, the effect is felt immediately by the person being forgiven no matter how far away he or she may be.

Returning to our situation with the mediators, we can think of the situation they most often find themselves in as a morphic field in which the individuals are held together, through morphic resonance, by a victim consciousness. As soon as one member (the mediator) shifts his consciousness in the direction of love and acceptance of what is, as is, the field immediately undergoes a transformation and evolves into a new vibratory arrangement of a higher order. Through morphic resonance, the other members of the group have an opportunity to become realigned in the same way, and the situation can evolve on completely different lines from the way it would have had the consciousness not been transformed in this way.

I mention Sheldrake's work to show that the way we talk about energy and consciousness has a firm foundation in modern scientific research and theory.

*Nelson Mandela Has Shown Us How*
The way Nelson Mandela handled the South African situation when apartheid finally ended in the early 1990s is an object lesson in how to transform energy through Radical Forgiveness. Apartheid, the white-dominated political system that had been in place for

three-quarters of a century, kept blacks and whites separated—the whites in luxury and the blacks in terrible
poverty. Mandela himself was imprisoned for twenty-
six years. Upon his release, he became president of
the country. South Africa was ripe for a bloodbath
of revenge, yet Mandela brought about an amazingly
peaceful transition—the hallmark of which was not
revenge but forgiveness.

It was not so much what he did that prevented the
predicted bloodbath from occurring, but how he handled
the energy. He refused to take revenge, and on behalf of
all the people he transcended the victim archetype. This,
in turn, collapsed the energy pattern of potential vio-
lence already in place and waiting to be triggered. South
Africa remains in transition today and not without problems, but it has progressed much farther than we could
have dreamed possible a few decades ago.

Our collective mission to transform the victim
archetype demands that we all follow Mandela's lead
and move beyond the experience of victimhood. If we
do not, we will stay hopelessly addicted to our woundedness and to the victim archetype.

*Spirit Nudges*
Deep inside our subconscious mind, we are in touch
with our mission. Spirit keeps presenting opportunities

to transform the victim energy by bringing things like incest, child abuse, sexual abuse, and racial hatred to the surface. Each one of us can embrace this mission by practicing Radical Forgiveness in any of these situations. If achieved by enough of us, the shift in perception that allows us to see the perfection in the situation will transform it so that the need for such energy patterns disappears.

*Exercise in Transformation*

To transform the victim archetype, practice the following: Every time you watch the news, shift your consciousness from one of judgment to one of seeing the perfection in the situation. Instead of accepting at face value a story about racial prejudice, for example, help transform the energy of racial disharmony. Do so by looking at the person or situation that would ordinarily receive your judgment and censure and see if instead you can move into a space of loving acceptance. Know that the people in the story are living out their part in the divine plan. Do not see anyone as a victim and refuse to label anyone a villain. People are just acting in dramas being played out so that healing can occur. Remember, God does not make mistakes!

# 12  The Ego Fights Back

By REMINDING US that we are spiritual beings having a human experience, Radical Forgiveness raises our vibration and moves us in the direction of spiritual evolution.

Such growth represents a real threat to the ego (defined here as the deep-seated, complex belief system that says we are separated from God and that He will one day punish us for choosing that separation). This is because the more spiritually evolved we become, the more likely it is that we will remember who we are—and that we are one with God.

Once we have this realization, the ego must die. If there is one thing we know about belief systems of any kind, they resist all attempts at making them wrong—and the ego is no exception. (People demonstrate all the time that they would rather be right than happy.)

Therefore, the more we use Radical Forgiveness, the more the ego fights back and tries to seduce us into remaining addicted to the victim archetype. One way it accomplishes this task is by using our own tools of spiritual growth. A good example of this is found in the ego's use of "inner child work" to keep us stuck in victimhood.

Inner child work gives us a way to look within and heal the wounds of childhood that we still carry within us as adults and that continue to affect our lives today. In our focus on our woundedness, however, the ego sees an opportunity. It exploits the kind of inner child work that uses the inner child as a metaphor for our woundedness, in order to strengthen our attachment to the victim archetype. The behavior this gives rise to is the constant revisiting of our wounds, giving them power through constantly speaking about them, projecting them onto a so-called inner child, and using them as the means to finding intimacy.

Much of the inner child work of the 1980s focused heavily on blaming our parents, or someone else, for the fact that we were unhappy as adults. The idea "I would be happy today if it weren't for my parents" is the mantra associated with this work. It gives us permission to feel that "they did this to us," a perception that is much easier to live with than believing that we have somehow *requested* to be treated in this manner. Such a viewpoint automatically recreates us as victim. As long as we continue to blame our parents for our problems, each succeeding generation continues this belief pattern.

I do not wish to imply that getting in touch with our repressed childhood rage and pain and finding ways to release it are bad. In fact, doing so is essential. We must first do this work before moving on to forgiveness, for we cannot forgive if we are angry. But too many workshops and therapies focus purely on the anger and fail to help us transform it through forgiveness of any kind. When we couple anger work with Radical Forgiveness, all sorts of repressed emotional and mental toxicity are cleared and the permanent release of anger becomes possible. Thus we move out of woundedness and beyond victimhood.

## THE NAVAJO FORGIVENESS RITUAL

I once heard Caroline Myss, author of *Why People Don't Heal and How They Can*, describe the ritual that the Navajo used for preventing woundology from becoming an addictive pattern. While they certainly recognized the need for people to speak of their wounds and to have them witnessed by the group, they understood that speaking about their wounds gave the wounds power, especially when done to excess. Therefore, if a person had a wound or a grievance to share, the tribe would meet and the person could bring it to the circle. This person was allowed to air his grievance three times, and everyone listened with empathy and compassion.

On the fourth occasion, however, as the person came into the circle, everyone turned their backs. "Enough! We have heard you express your concern three times. We have received it. Now let it go. We will not hear it again," they said. This served as a powerful ritual of support for letting go of past pain.

Imagine what would happen if we were to support our friends in that same manner. What if, after they had complained about their wounds and their victimization three times, we then said, "I have heard you enough on this subject. It's time you let it go. I will not give your wounds power over you any longer by allowing you to talk about them to me. I love you too much."

I am sure that if we did this, many of our friends would call us traitors. They would likely see our behavior not as an act of pure, loving support but of betrayal, and they might turn against us immediately.

If we are to truly support each other on the journey of spiritual evolution, we have no choice but to take the risk, draw a line in the sand with those we love, and do our best to gently help move them beyond their addiction to their wounds. Such action will lead us to the achievement of our collective missions to transform the victim archetype and to remember who we really are.

# 13 Time, Medicine, and Forgiveness

SPIRITUAL EVOLUTION BRINGS with it a new appreciation for and knowledge of our physical bodies and how to care for them. The medical paradigm we have held for the last three hundred years—ever since the French philosopher René Descartes defined the body as a machine—is changing radically as it moves toward a holistic, mind-body approach.

We used to think of health as the absence of disease. Now we think of it in terms of how well our life force (prana, chi, etc.) flows through our bodies. For optimum health, this life force must be able to flow freely. We cannot be healthy if our bodies are clogged with the energy of resentment, anger, sadness, guilt, and grief.

When we speak here of the body, we include not only the physical body, which is also an energy body, but the subtle bodies that surround us as well. These we refer to individually as the etheric body, the emotional body, the mental body, and the causal body.

Each has a different frequency. Whereas we used to define the physical body in terms of chemicals and molecules, physicists have taught us to see all five bodies, including the physical one, as dense condensations of interacting energy patterns.

The subtle fields envelop the physical body in layers like vibrating sheaths of energy, each one an octave higher than the previous. But they are not fixed bands with clear boundaries, as shown in Figure 10. Rather, they are to a large degree diffused within the same space, as if they were all part of an ocean of energy surrounding our bodies. The subtle bodies are not so much defined by their position in space as by the different frequencies at which they vibrate.

The subtle bodies resonate harmonically with the vibrating patterns of the physical body, enabling consciousness (mind) to interact with the body. This is what we mean when we speak of the *body-mind continuum*, with mind existing both inside and outside the physical body. (For more details on the qualities and purpose ascribed to each of these subtle bodies, refer to Chapter 15.)

To ground this concept in a practical analogy, think of our bodies as being like the filters typically found in home heating furnaces—the kind we have to clean from time to time to ensure the furnace works

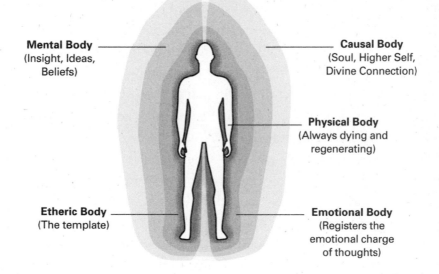

FIGURE 10  **The Subtle Energy Bodies**

efficiently. Just as these filters are designed to allow air to move easily through them, the same is true of our bodies and the life force. Life force must be free to flow easily through all our bodies—our physical one and our subtle bodies too.

Whenever we judge, make someone wrong, blame, project, repress anger, hold resentment, and the like, we create an energy block in our body/bodies. Each time

155

we do this, our filter becomes a little more blocked and less energy remains available for our furnace. Sooner or later the filter fails, and, starved of the vital oxygen it must have to keep burning, the flame dies. More simply, when our physical and subtle bodies become too clogged for life force to flow through easily, our body starts to shut down. In many cases, this manifests first as depression. Eventually, our body gets sick, and, if the blocks are not removed, we may die.

You may recall how my sister, Jill, felt a release of energy when she moved into Radical Forgiveness. Her life force filter was blocked by her toxic belief system about her own lack of worthiness, not to mention past resentments, anger, sadness, and frustration over her current situation. When she let all that go, her energy blocks were cleared, which allowed her to shift her emotional state as well. Whenever you forgive radically, you release enormous amounts of life force energy that then can be made available for healing, creativity, and expressing your true purpose in life.

### Farra's Flu Release

My good friend Farra Allen, co-founder of the Atlanta School of Massage and a mind/body counselor, took ill with a particularly virulent strain of flu that typically keeps people in bed for ten days or more. It hit him hard, but instead of giving all his power to the virus, he decided to do some inner work around it, work that might shift the energy pattern holding the virus in place. Using a process known as active imagination, which simply involves writing down thoughts as a stream of consciousness, he came upon a hitherto unconscious and unresolved emotional issue. He used Radical Forgiveness to clear the issue, and the flu disappeared almost immediately. He was working full time and feeling great within two days of the onset of his illness. This was a powerful demonstration of the healing power of Radical Forgiveness.

*Will Cancer Respond Too?*

Suppose the illness had been cancer rather than the flu, and it was our belief that it had started as a deeply repressed emotion. Thinking the cure might lie in releasing that energy block, our recommendation would have have been that my friend get in touch with the repressed feelings, feel them fully, and then let them go.

However, unlike Farra's flu attack, which probably moved from his subtle body into his physical body in just a few days, this energy pattern might have taken many years to move from the subtle body into the physical body and, in time, to manifest as a disease.

The question that haunts us then becomes, how long will it take for the disease process to fully reverse itself using emotional release work alone? Conceivably, it could require the same number of years it took for the disease to manifest—not very practical if you have cancer or some other disease for which time is of the essence—or so it might seem, anyway.

### Time Is a Factor in Healing

We used to think of time as something fixed and linear, until Einstein showed that time is a relative concept. In terms of how long it takes to heal a physical disease or condition, consciousness is definitely a factor. The more elevated our consciousness, the faster we create change in anything to which we give our focused attention.

Think of consciousness as our vibratory rate. It would probably take far too long to reverse the disease process of cancer energetically in a person with a low vibratory rate. It will automatically be low if we are in fear, hold anger and resentment, think of ourselves as a victim, and/or have our energy locked up in the past. For the majority of us, this represents our consciousness most of the time. Therefore, few of us could reverse a disease like cancer fast enough by relying solely on releasing the emotional cause of the disease—that is, unless we can find a way to raise our vibratory rate.

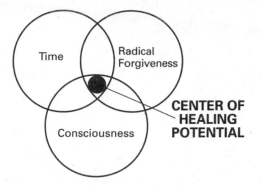

Figure 11  **Time and Healing**

By letting go of the victim archetype and bringing our energy into present time through the process of Radical Forgiveness, we may be able to raise our vibration enough to create at least a quicker, if not immediate, disease reversal. We improve our chances if we also incorporate other ways of raising our vibration, such as prayer and meditation.

Here is an example. A woman who attended one of our retreats had had several surgeries for ovarian cancer, and her doctors had recently given her three months at the most to live. She was depressed and had little life force left. She said she only came to the retreat because the people in her church had collected the money for her to come, so she felt obliged to do so. We worked with her, and on the third day she had a wonderful breakthrough that put her in touch with an

159

event that had occurred when she was two-and-a-half years old and had made her believe herself to be utterly worthless. She released a lot of emotion around that issue and grieved for the countless number of times she had created her life in ways that proved her worthlessness. After that, her life force energy increased. By the time she left, she was all fired up to find an alternative program that would help her beat the cancer and the doctor's prognosis. She was even willing to travel outside the U.S. if the method she chose was illegal in this country. (Many treatments are illegal in the U.S.)

After two weeks of frantically searching for the treatment to which she felt most drawn, she suddenly realized that her healing would come through prayer. So she went away to a place in upstate New York and worked with a couple who offered prayer weeks: she literally prayed for a week. Upon her return, she went to her oncologist, who examined her and said, "I don't know how to explain this, but you have absolutely no cancer in your body. I could say it was a spontaneous remission, but I believe in God, and I am not willing to describe it in any other way than as a miracle."

This woman serves as a wonderful example of how raising the vibration through prayer reversed the physical condition in days rather than years. I believe that Radical Forgiveness would have done the same.

### Seattle Forgiveness Study

An interesting but as yet unpublished study on for-giveness and time was conducted at Seattle University. It involved a series of interviews with people who, by their own assessment, had been victimized. The researchers wanted to see how that perception changed over time. Preliminary findings showed that seren-ity, which was described as "having no resentment left," came *not* through any act of forgiveness but as a sudden *discovery* that the participants had indeed for-given. All reported that the more they tried to forgive, the harder it became and the more resentment they felt. They stopped trying to forgive and *just let go*. After varying intervals of time came the surprising realiza-tion that they no longer harbored resentment and that they had, in fact, forgiven.

A later and even more interesting discovery revealed that the realization that they had forgiven was pre-ceded by being forgiven themselves. (Who forgave them and for what was irrelevant.) What this certainly points to is that forgiveness is a shift in energy. Having experienced being forgiven—a release of stuck energy—they were able to release their own stuck energy with someone else vitually automatically.

This study not only reinforces the insight that forgive-ness cannot be willed but also shows that forgiveness happens as an internal transformation through a combination of surrendering one's attachment to resentment and accepting forgiveness for oneself. The study's results also underscore the value of step nine in the twelve-step process used successfully by millions of people in Alcoholics Anonymous and other similar programs. Step nine asks that we seek to make amends to those we have harmed and that we ask them for forgiveness. When we find that we have in fact been forgiven, this frees our own energy to forgive not only others but ourselves as well.

Some might argue that the Seattle study illustrates the slowness of the forgiveness process and shows that forgiveness would offer a rather ineffective method for curing a disease such as cancer. In many cases, it took people decades to discover that they had forgiven.

The important distinction to make, however, is that the study did not distinguish between Radical Forgiveness and traditional forgiveness. What it described was definitely the latter. I would be willing to wager that, if the subject group had been divided into two—one group with insight into Radical Forgiveness and the other left basically to use traditional forgiveness—the group with the additional insight would have reached the state of serenity infinitely more quickly than the other group.

I am not claiming that Radical Forgiveness always occurs instantaneously either—though I have to say I have seen it happen instantaneously many times now. Neither can it be claimed as a definitive cure for cancer. However, it certainly should be an integral part of any treatment protocol. Sometimes people even delay medical treatment to see if Radical Forgiveness creates enough of an effect to make such drastic intervention unnecessary. That would be unthinkable with traditional forgiveness.

### Mary's Story

My friend Mary, a co-facilitator at many of my retreats, denied for months that something was terribly wrong with her health. When she could not ignore the obvious any longer, she went to a doctor who told her she had stage three colon cancer—they wanted to operate immediately. She asked them for thirty days, and they reluctantly agreed. She went to a little cabin in the mountains and stayed there for a week, meditating and working on forgiving all the people in her life, including herself, using Radical Forgiveness. She fasted, prayed, cried, and literally went through the dark night of the soul. She came back home and worked with several practitioners to cleanse her body and strengthen her immune system.

At the end of the thirty-day period, the surgery was performed. Afterward, her doctor wanted to know what she had done, for the cancer had all but disappeared and, instead of the radical surgery they had said would be necessary, removal of the cancer required only minor intervention.

In cases where the disease is so advanced or aggressive as to require immediate medical intervention, surgery, chemotherapy, or radiation buy time. But time for what?

Remember: there is no cure for cancer. Consequently, no matter what the medical treatment, doctors have an unspoken expectation that a recurrence is almost a foregone conclusion and just a question of time. I prefer to look at the treatment, assuming the patient survives it, as a way to buy the time to do the Radical Forgiveness work that could actually prevent any recurrence.

Radical Forgiveness provides one of the best preventive measures available. It clears the energy in the subtle bodies long before it becomes a block in the physical body. When I help people resolve forgiveness issues by using Radical Forgiveness Therapy, as I did with my sister, Jill, I believe I am not only helping them heal a wound in their subtle body but also helping them prevent disease occurring in the physical body. I am convinced that if we keep the energy flowing in our bodies as it was designed to do, we will never get sick. Though I no longer do the five-day cancer retreats I used to, I nevertheless regard the Radical Forgiveness workshops that I now present all around the world as cancer prevention workshops.

Of course, adequate exercise, good diet, and other such common-sense practices help in this regard as well. But keeping our energy bodies clear of emotional dross and toxicity is of primary importance to good health and healing. Unfortunately, this aspect of healing gets the least media attention, despite the fact that, in America alone, one out of every five people takes an antidepressant drug such as Prozac. Bearing in mind that depression always precedes cancer, we have to wonder whether it is mere coincidence that one out of five Americans also dies of cancer.

I am often asked why I work with people who have cancer. I have had no personal experience with it, and I knew little about it from a medical standpoint when I began offering five-day cancer retreats for emotional and spiritual healing in the early 1990s.

It was only after doing this work for some time that I realized why I was attracted to it: it was because it linked up with my interest in forgiveness. This insight occurred when I discovered that nearly all cancer patients, besides having a lifetime habit of suppressing and repressing emotions, are known to share a marked inability to forgive.

I now believe that lack of forgiveness contributes to, and may even be a principal cause of, most cancers. Therefore, my healing work with cancer patients, and with those who want to prevent the disease from arising or recurring in their bodies, now centers almost entirely on Radical Forgiveness Therapy.

## Jane's Story

Jane came to one of our five-day retreats in the north Georgia mountains. She had had a mastectomy and was awaiting a bone marrow transplant. After the retreat, she came to me once a week for hypnotherapy and individual coaching. On the second visit, she arrived in a distressed state, because a routine MRI scan had that day discovered minute spots of cancer in her brain. While this new cancer was upsetting enough by itself, its appearance was also liable to spoil her chances of a transplant. The doctors planned to give her chemotherapy to try to arrest the cancer's progress, but they were surprised at her condition, because normally metastasis proceeds from the breast to the liver and then to the brain; very rarely does it move directly from the breast to the brain. To me, this seemed worthy of some exploration.

Jane was an attractive woman in her early forties who had not been involved in a romantic relationship for about seven years. She had a boyfriend of sorts, but she described the relationship as not much more than a close friendship. In fact, she said, she looked upon him as her buddy, even though she had sex with him from time to time. As I probed further into her relationship situation, she got in touch with some incredible grief she still felt around a relationship she had ended a number of years earlier. This eight-year relationship had been extremely passionate and intense, and Jane clearly worshipped the man. Four years into the relationship, which she believed was soon to be consummated in marriage, she discovered that he was married already and had children. He had no intention of leaving his wife. Jane was devastated but could not stop seeing him. It took her another four extremely painful years to extricate herself from the relationship.

It was clear to me that as a result of this failed relationship, Jane had shut down her emotions completely and would no longer allow herself to get involved so deeply with a man. Neither was I surprised that she had suffered a broken heart; most women with breast cancer have a broken heart somewhere in their history. (The breast is the organ of nurturance and is in the proximity of, and related to, the heart.)

As she was going out the door at the end of our session, Jane said in a whisper, "I put him in the attic."

I stopped in my tracks. "What do you mean?" I asked.

"Well, everything I had accumulated over the years that had any connection to this man, or that would remind me of him, I stuffed in a box. I then put the box up in the attic. It's still there. I haven't touched it since."

I told her to sit down and tell me that again. I had her repeat the same thing three times. Suddenly, she saw the connection between the box in the attic that represented her broken love affair and her brain cancer. "Oh, my God," she said. "That's him in my head, isn't it? He's in my attic."

I told her to go home, go up into the attic, take down the box, and bring it with her to her next session. We would go through it piece by piece together. We planned for her to tell me the story behind each item until we had exorcised his energy and released the pain she had repressed. Jane understood that this might be the key to her healing and was very excited. Tragically, she had a seizure the next day and was taken back to the hospital. She died a month later without ever touching the box in the attic. Looking at the box's contents and feeling the pain of her lost love may have been just too much for her to bear, and I feel that, at some level, she may have decided to let go of life rather than face that pain.

## ORIGINS OF ILLNESS

Energy blocks always begin in the subtle bodies first. Then, if they are not released at that level, they move into the physical body and ultimately manifest as diseases such as cancer, multiple sclerosis, diabetes, and the like. Thus, we can say that illness always begins in the subtle bodies first and moves inward.

We used to think that the best way to stay ahead of disease was to visit a medical doctor for regular checkups. We now know that we are much better off consulting with people who can read our auras—meaning that they can tune in to the energy patterns of our subtle bodies, particularly the etheric body. They can see blocks building energetically long before they show up in the physical body. Medical intuitives can do the same.

There are now also sophisticated technological diagnostic systems that do this. Called electrodermal screening devices, they are mostly used by naturopaths, homeopaths, osteopaths, and chiropractors. The machine uses the acupuncture points (which are in the etheric body) to get readings on each organ system of the body and to register disease at the subclinical level. These are proving to be very accurate devices, though as yet most medical doctors fail to recognize their efficacy. Healing a disease pattern in the subtle body proves much easier than waiting for it to condense into physical matter, because once it does that, it becomes much more resistant to change.

Quantum physicists have actually proven that emotions condense as energy particles that, if not expressed as emotion, become lodged in the spaces between atoms and molecules. This is literally the filter becoming clogged. Once the emotion has become a particle, it becomes much more difficult to release, and therein lies the problem. It takes much more time and effort to release that block from the physical body than it would have if it had been released while still in pure energy form in the subtle body/bodies—in this case, the emotional body.

It is possible, however, to shift those particles before they do harm, and the best way I know to do so involves a combination of Radical Forgiveness and Satori Breathwork. (See Chapter 27.) But if those particles are left to accumulate and coagulate into a mass that one day becomes a cancer, the problem becomes highly intractable and subsequently life-threatening.

## WHY WE DON'T HEAL

Clearly, time and healing are directly related. For us to evolve to the extent that we can heal ourselves, we must have most of our consciousness in present time—not in

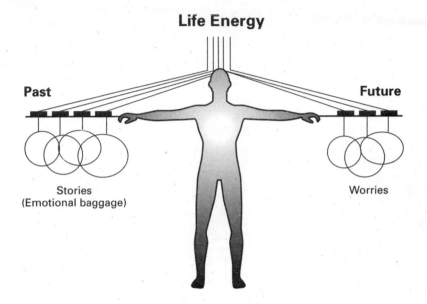

**Life Energy**

**Past**

**Future**

Stories
(Emotional baggage)

Worries

Figure 12　**Why People Don't Heal**

the past, not in the future, but in the *now*. In her tape series *Why People Don't Heal*, Caroline Myss maintains that people with more than 60 percent of their life energy siphoned off to maintain the past are unable to heal themselves energetically. Thus they remain totally reliant upon chemical medicine for their healing.

Myss argues that if it takes 60 to 70 percent of the average person's precious life force to manage the negative experiences of his or her childhood, adolescence, and earlier years of adulthood, as well as to hold on

171

to the losses, disappointments, and resentments of the past, and another 10 percent to worry about, plan for, and try to control the future. That leaves precious little energy for the present moment—or for healing. (It is important to note that it does not drain our energy to maintain positive memories or even negative memories if they have been processed and forgiven.)

Life has its own way of bringing us—and our energy—into present time. Often it occurs through trauma. When we find ourselves in the midst of a disaster, have an unexpected accident, or discover that our lives are suddenly in danger, we become very focused on the present moment. We bring all our consciousness into the present instinctively, and suddenly the past does not matter, nor does the future. Only this moment exists. The power of such currently focused energy is demonstrated when a mother, seeing her child trapped under a car, suddenly becomes able to lift the car off the ground so her child can be rescued. Acts of incredible bravery and courage also happen when energy becomes focused in the moment, because fear only occurs when we bring the past into the future. When we are truly in the moment we are absolutely fearless, because we have no awareness of past or future.

Radical Forgiveness helps us to be in present time because we do not forgive radically by going back into the past. We simply forgive the person who happens to be mirroring our projection right here in the present. That is the beauty of Radical Forgiveness. It is true that sometimes the past connection will be so clear that, as in Jill's case, it illuminates the current situation. But the focus is still on the perfection of what is happening *in the now.*

We can either choose to let go of the victim archetype and bring our energy into the present through Radical Forgiveness or wait for a significant trauma to force us into the now. In other words, we can either transform our consciousness as a matter of will or we can wait for a disaster or a life-threatening illness to make us do it.

# 14 As Above, So Below

HUMANITY AS A whole may soon be faced with the same choice that confronts each one of us as individuals. As I pointed out in the previous chapter, the decision is to heal by choice or by trauma.

Many visionaries claim that all the signs are present that point toward humankind receiving a massive demonstration of the heal-by-choice-or-trauma principle in the very near future. The Earth has a cancer, and it is called the human race. This living, breathing, conscious planet has been in a state of perfect balance its entire life, with every little part doing what it must to sustain the system in balance. This is analogous to the job done by healthy cells in the human body.

For thousands of years we have been part of that balanced system. In the last few hundred of them, however, we have put ourselves above the natural order and have come to believe that we can control and dominate the entire system. Just as a cancer cell multiplies out of control, metastasizes throughout the system, and begins to devour its host, so we continue to multiply exponentially out of control all over the planet and to plunder its natural resources as if nothing mattered beyond the satisfaction of our greed.

Like a tumor wrapping itself around the heart or blocking a lung, so do we, in the same kind of deadly embrace with our own life source, chop down forests, pollute the very air we breathe, and poison the environment. Scientists are telling us that we are close to destroying life as we know it within the next forty to fifty years if we don't make dramatic changes.

The greatest need, however, is for a change in consciousness. Collectively, we must change mass consciousness or face unprecedented trauma at such a level that all the structures maintaining our present lifestyle will be swept away.

## EARTH CHANGES
## AND POLITICAL UPHEAVAL

From earliest times right up to the present, massive and disastrous earth changes have been predicted for the early years of the new millennium. Predictions include two polar shifts, dramatic earthquakes, drastically altered weather patterns, volcanic eruptions, and a significant rise in sea levels as polar ice caps melt.

The result of such events would be a radically changed map of the world, with much of what we see today as land disappearing under water and new continents rising from the sea. The disruption and chaos would be unimaginable, and millions of people would die. Political upheavals, religious wars, and environmental damage would also occur on a massive scale.

Such predictions were most notably made by the famous seer of the sixteenth century, Nostradamus, and in this century by Edgar Cayce, the "sleeping prophet" who made very precise predictions in the 1940s. They also appear in many religious writings, including the Bible's Book of Revelation and in the traditional texts of the Mayans, the Hopi Indians, and many other indigenous peoples.

It is clear to many that these earth changes have already begun. As the effects of global warming become impossible to ignore, the scientific community is making its own series of predictions based on the worldwide increase in floods, droughts, hurricanes, tornadoes, and volcanic eruptions, all of which bear close resemblance to the predictions of Cayce and others. Just recently, the world has become a whole lot more unstable politically, and some of what is happening looks uncomfortably like what has been predicted.

## Consciousness Counts

Scientists do not talk much about the effects of consciousness on the earth, preferring instead to focus on what action we should take to prevent impending doom. But the more spiritually oriented predictions have always carried with them the caveat that the severity of earth changes and political upheaval may be mitigated to the extent that we human beings come to our senses and change our consciousness. In other words, even though our fear/greed-based consciousness has wounded the etheric body of the planet so badly that a violent eruption in its physical form seems inevitable, we can still lessen the effect by raising our consciousness. Just as a disease pattern in the etheric body of a human being can be healed by nonphysical means (prayer, Reiki, imagery, hands-on healing, Radical Forgiveness Therapy, etc.), so the pattern of upheaval and violent change already set in the earth's etheric body can be dissipated before it manifests in the physical. The answer seems to be, amazingly enough, prayer.

Science has been putting the spotlight on prayer over the last few years, and there is a growing consensus in that community that it actually works. We truly create our reality through our prayers. Not the kind of prayers, I hasten to add, that consist of requests or demands that God give us this or that, or make this happen rather than that, or in some other way tell God what to do.

No, the essence of creative prayer is not a matter of words or thoughts. It is actually *feeling*. Prayer will manifest what you want only when you are able to be fully in the feeling of having it already, knowing that it is done, or that you have already been gifted with it. A feeling of profound gratitude is perhaps the nearest one can come to describing it.

But even this is tied to a particular outcome and probably will not raise the consciousness sufficiently high to shift the energy to the degree required.

The purest form of prayer we can engage in is to feel peace: the kind of peace that comes when we surrender totally to what is, as is—in the knowledge and comfort that Spirit has it all handled and that it will all work out for the best if we just get ourselves out of the way.

It is only when we are fully surrendered to the situation we are in that the energy will open up for changes to occur—and what they will be, heaven only knows! Don't pray *for* peace. Pray to *feel* peace. That's the most creative prayer you can make. Peace is the strongest power on earth, and it is certainly called for at this time. When we can feel peace in our hearts, we will know love and our world will reflect it.

This means that we have a choice. Each individual can make a choice to stay in the feeling of fear, lack, mistrust, greed, and guilt, or choose to let go of all that and be in peace. It is as simple as that. Peace/love is the only antidote to the fear-based consciousness that we now live in and participate in daily. So simply choose it. We have the technology. Use Radical Forgiveness daily in order to make that choice real— and see what happens!

What we may be seeing at this time is the earth and all of humankind going through a healing crisis—and it may have to get worse before it gets better. (A healing crisis occurs when an organism goes through what looks like a dramatic worsening of its condition, such as with a fever or an eruption of boils, just before it starts to get well again. This worsened condition serves as a cleansing and detoxification process.)

No matter how drastic things get, we must believe that perfection and divine purpose exist even in this kind of situation. After all, who could possibly have imagined a more dramatic way for Spirit to lovingly mirror our own lust for control and greed than this? Or to mirror our need to create separation between people? We cannot evolve spiritually while holding onto these energies, and if it takes earth changes to bring us to a healing of them, so be it. The planet will be healed in the process. So, too, will we.

To put this whole discussion in perspective, we must also keep in mind that, since the physical world is actually an illusion, what we experience as earth changes will be illusionary too. This explains why a change in human consciousness can change the situation immediately. The way we experience earth changes depends upon our perception of what is happening. If we see them as a purification of consciousness and a healing crisis that will result in a spiritual transformation, our experience of them will be in stark contrast to what we will feel if we take the victim position and think of them as real, as things to be feared, and as a punishment for our rank stupidity. A Radical Forgiveness perspective will enable us to stay focused on the perfection of what is happening in the moment and will carry us through to the joy and peace on the other side of the experience.

## The Gift

The adage "as above, so below" is meaningful, too, in terms of how we respond to both the cancer in our bodies and the cancer on the planet. Waging "war" on cancer with toxic drugs and other violent treatment will never bring about a cure for cancer. Violent, high-tech, politically motivated solutions to the earth's problems won't work either. The only thing that will work, in both cases, is *love*. When we really comprehend this, we will have understood the gift of both earth changes and cancer.

No lesson is more crucial than this one. People with cancer are brave souls who have come to the physical plane with a mission to demonstrate the futility of projecting anger and war on the body and on ourselves. Their mission is to help us understand that the only answer to any situation is *love*. Our gift in return is to hear their loving message.

*Visions of Joy, Harmony, and Peace*

Whether or not we raise our vibration sufficiently to prevent trauma and come into loving resonance with all of life voluntarily, the end result will ultimately be the same. All the predictions about earth changes speak of a breakthrough in consciousness happening in the wake of the earth cleansing itself and balancing the karma we have created.

A vision of life after the earth changes as wonderfully harmonious, peaceful, and idyllic, in stark contrast to the way it is today, is a common theme running through many of the predictions. As in all healing opportunities, we can heal our soul pain at the first sign of the repressed pain occurring, or we can wait until a disaster wakes us. However the earth changes occur and at whatever level of destruction the planetary karma plays out, the changes will constitute the ultimate healing crisis for the planet and for all of us. That will certainly be in divine order.

Raising our vibration enough to change the predictions must include living our lives based on love and gentle acceptance of ourselves and others and forgiving ourselves for abusing the planet. It must include joining in prayer for peace, with as many people as possible from around the world involved, and embracing Radical Forgiveness as nothing less than a permanent way of life.

*part three*

---

# Assumptions Expanded

# 15  Articles of Faith

THE ASSUMPTIONS LISTED in Chapter 2 were made briefly, to give you just enough of an understanding of them to comprehend the theory of Radical Forgiveness. Now I would like to discuss in greater depth the assumptions underlying Radical Forgiveness that have not yet been comprehensively discussed. I hope this will help you find a level of comfort with them, even if you cannot entirely accept them.

Remember, all theories are based upon assumptions, but not all assumptions are proven with evidence of their validity. This holds especially true for theories and assumptions pertaining to the nature of reality and spiritual issues.

Interestingly, science and mysticism have come to a new level of agreement about the nature of reality and other spiritual questions that until now have seemed beyond the reach of science. For centuries, Hindu mystics have claimed to possess a "direct knowing" of these universal truths, which they assert they have arrived at as a result of forty years of meditating in Himalayan caves. By using rigorous scientific methods and theoretical constructs, scientists have recently arrived at the same truths—or, should we say, have made similar assumptions. It is now safe to say that quantum physics actually demonstrates the truth of what the mystics have known for centuries. How exciting it is to see a joining of these two distinct ways of approaching and arriving at truth. Science and spirituality have come together at last, with scientists becoming modern-day mystics!

Yet in spite of the progress we have made, in all humility we must continue to keep in mind that these assumptions, by their very nature, do not represent the whole truth. The great mysteries of how the universe works and of the higher purpose of human life still lie beyond mere mortal understanding, and the assumptions we make are mere approximations of what might be the truth. On this basis, therefore, the following assumptions are given as the foundation for Radical Forgiveness.

**Assumption:** Contrary to most Western religious thought, we are not human beings having an occasional spiritual experience. Rather, we are spiritual beings having a human experience.

This is not just a play on words. It represents a fundamental shift in our thinking about who we are and our relationship with God. Instead of thinking of ourselves as fallen and separated from God, it suggests that we are still very much connected to the All That Is, and that life in a physical body is just a temporary interlude taken for the purpose of learning and balancing energy. It also suggests that God lives within each of us rather than "up there", highlighting our dual man/spirit nature. Pulitzer Prize-winner Ernst Becker explained this vividly by saying, "Man is a God who shits."[2]

**Assumption:** We have physical bodies that die, but we are immortal.

For centuries philosophers have debated the makeup of the "soul." This discussion predates even Plato and Socrates, both of whom had much to say about the soul but remained very much at odds on the subject. Today, the debate continues, with little agreement on what constitutes the soul.

For the purposes of this discussion, however, the soul is defined as the part of us that is pure consciousness connected to the greater ocean of consciousness that forms the All That Is. For the purposes of our

189

incarnation, the soul takes on an individual charac-
teristic that can be likened to a single droplet of that
same ocean or a little bit of God Stuff. Since we are
a part of the ocean of the All That Is, we have always
existed as a soul. The soul has no beginning and no
end, exists outside of both time and space, and is
immortal. During our incarnation, the soul keeps us
connected to the World of Divine Truth and the All
That Is and is responsible for our spiritual evolution.

Once the soul incarnates, it becomes attached to
both a body and a personality, which together represent
a "persona" or identity. This we create for ourselves
based on our own self-concept, which we present to the
world at large. Thus our soul becomes subject to the
stresses of human existence and can even become sick.
A great many of the sicknesses of today, such as cancer,
begin as a deep sickness of the soul. Shamans speak
of the soul becoming fractured and splintered, parts
of it actually being left behind and lost in past events,
especially traumas. A great deal of a shaman's healing
work revolves around the idea of soul retrieval.

Whether a soul incarnates just once or does so
over and over again has been an issue of contention
through the ages, and many churches and religions
will not consider this idea even today. Yet Eastern religions have always included reincarnation among their

spiritual beliefs. I do not regard reincarnation as central to Radical Forgiveness, and it is of no consequence whether one believes it or not. It has no effect on the efficacy of Radical Forgiveness and is simply a matter of personal choice. (If the idea of reincarnation offends you, skip the next couple of pages.)

For myself, I am not attached either way, although there does seem to be evidence to support the idea, especially through the vast amount of writing about near-death experiences. These accounts are so similar in their content and quality they can hardly be refuted. Thousands of people have reported similar kinds of experiences and exhibit the same degree of certainty that what they saw was real. The effects near-death experiences have on people's lives are more or less identical as well.

From this same source, it appears that not only do our souls incarnate numerous times but that they do not come into this physical life experience alone. Past life research seems to suggest that our souls keep coming back time and time again with others from our soul group to resolve particular karmic imbalances.

During our journey toward wholeness, we create energy imbalances that have to be resolved. These imbalances are referred to as our karma. For example, if we take advantage of people and cheat them, we must at some time have the experience of being cheated to equalize the energy. This is not a moral exercise; it has nothing to do with right or wrong. As I have already noted, the Universe is neutral. This happens simply as a balancing of energy and is dictated by the Law of Cause and Effect, which states that for every action there must be an equal reaction. (See Chapter 9.)

The people with whom we play and the games we play with them are all about balancing energy in this manner. Our soul heals and becomes whole again each time we rebalance the karmic energies. Thus, each incarnation contributes to the healing of the soul.

Incidentally, since time does not exist in the World of Divine Truth, all our incarnations happen simultaneously. As we heal in one lifetime, we heal all the other incarnations as well. Using Radical Forgiveness in one lifetime, therefore, provides incredible value to a soul because it heals all the other incarnations at the same time as it heals the current one. Imagine the collective karma that was balanced by Nelson Mandela forgiving a whole generation of whites in South Africa for their treatment of blacks. By the same token, imagine the collective karma that remains to be balanced in the United States for the treatment of slaves and Native Americans.

Our soul always moves us in the direction of healing and keeps creating situations that offer us the opportunity to balance karmic energy. But if this healing is not accomplished at the level of Divine Truth, we tend to recreate the imbalance through the resentment and revenge cycle and the maintenance of victim consciousness. This keeps the wheel of karma spinning round and round and round. Radical Forgiveness provides one of the best ways to stop the wheel from turning, because it breaks the cycle.

Having said all that, if you have a problem with the concept of reincarnation, simply ignore it. It makes no difference.

**Assumption:** While our bodies and our senses tell us we are separate individuals, in truth we are all one. We all individually vibrate as part of a single whole.

We are not our bodies. We are not our personality selves or the roles we play each day. Believing we are these things serves to further reinforce our belief in separation. Upholding this belief prevents us—until we awaken, that is—from remembering who we really are: individual souls created as part of God and existing in oneness with God.

**Assumption:** When we were all one with God, we experimented with a thought that separation was possible. We became trapped in that thought, which became the dream that we now live. It is a dream because the separation did not actually happen. We only think it did—and that thought gave birth to the belief system we call the ego (the "as enemy" version).

Once we were completely enfolded in the All That Is—God. We were formless, unchanging, and immortal, and knew only love. Then we had a thought. What would it be like, we wondered, if we were to descend into physical reality and experience the opposite energies—such as form, change, separation, fear, death, limitation, and duality? We played with the idea for a while, always thinking we could withdraw from the experiment any time we wished, should we indeed decide to put the thought into action. We saw no danger. Thus, the decision was made, and we lowered our energetic vibration to condense our energy into physical form. In the process, we forgot our connection to God and imagined we had actually separated from God and that we had no way back to the All That Is.

This dream became very real for us, and we then became extremely guilt-ridden for committing this "original" sin of separating from God. We became fearful that God would bring His wrath down upon us for having done so. This powerful belief in sin, guilt, and fear became the ego, and it became such a powerful force in our lives that it created in our minds a world dominated by fear. Our world is still one where fear, rather than love, is the driving force.

Though we tend to personify it, the ego is not an entity in and of itself. Neither does it represent our personality. The ego represents a set of deeply held beliefs that keep us utterly convinced of our separateness from God. The extreme power exerted by these subconscious beliefs through the dynamics of guilt, fear, repression, and projection creates the appearance that the ego "lives" in us. The ego keeps us stuck in the World of Humanity and asleep (unconscious), dreaming that we have separated from God.

**Assumption:** When we decided to experiment with physical incarnation, God gave us total free will to live this experiment in any way we chose and to find for ourselves the way home to the All That Is.

Free will is honored at the highest level. Contrary to what some would have us believe, God is not mad at us for playing with the idea of separation. God gives us anything we want, whatever we choose, and makes no judgment about it. Whenever we ask for help through prayer and Radical Forgiveness, the call is always answered.

**Assumption:** Life is not a random event. It has purpose and provides for the unfolding of a divine plan, with opportunities to make choices and decisions in every moment.

Seen from the World of Humanity, it might appear that we arrive on this planet by biological accident. Our only significance lies in the fact that our parents made love and started a chain of biological events called pregnancy and birth.

It also might appear as if the only ways to master the experience of life are to learn a lot about how the world works and develop skills that enable us to control, as much as possible, the seemingly random circumstances of our lives. The more mastery we achieve over the physical circumstances of our lives, the better our lives appear to become.

The opposite is true when viewed from the World of Divine Truth. From this perspective, our arrival on the planet represents a deliberate, planned, and conscious choice. The plan includes the selection of the people who will serve as our parents.

Also, the seemingly haphazard events of our lives are attributed to the unfolding of a divine plan, decided upon in advance, and completely purposeful in terms of our spiritual growth. The more we surrender to this unfoldment without trying to control it, the more peaceful we become.

At first blush, this seems a fatalistic viewpoint, but this is not just fate. In truth, the divine plan allows for a great deal of creativity and flexibility and continues to honor the principle of free will. We continue to co-create with Spirit the circumstances of our lives and, without exception, to get precisely what we want. The extent to which we resist (judge) what we get determines whether we experience life as painful or joyful.

Mastery of the life experience, then, relies on our entering life fully and trusting that we are taken care of and supported all the time, no matter what. Radical Forgiveness moves us in that direction.

**Assumption:** Physical reality is an illusion created by our five senses. Matter consists of interrelating energy fields vibrating at different frequencies.

Most people have a difficult time coming to grips with the idea that our physical reality is an illusion created by our senses. Ken Carey confirms the difficulty we have grasping this concept. In his book *The Starseed Transmissions,* which was a channeled work, the souls "talking through him" made an interesting observation.[3]

They said that when they got inside Carey's body and experienced all his senses, they were simply amazed. Only then did they understand why human beings felt the physical world was real. Our senses make the illusion so convincing that even these disincarnate souls appreciated why we would have great difficulty getting beyond it. Indeed, it is difficult to remember that the physical world is simply an illusion.

However, we are beginning to move in a direction that fosters that memory. Recently, scientists have begun talking about the human body in terms of a mind/body continuum. Such terminology gives us the sense that our bodies are, indeed, more than cells, molecules, and atoms. Energy science tells us that, in reality, our bodies are dense condensations of interrelating energy fields and that, just like a hologram, all matter consists of energy vibrating in certain patterns. Holograms are those seemingly real, three-dimensional images created by laser beams. Quantum physicists have theorized that the entire universe is a hologram and everything in it, including each one of us, is a hologram as well.

Some energy fields vibrate at frequencies that enable them to be observed and measured. They can be given physical qualities like weight, volume, hardness, and fluidity. We give such energy patterns names like wood, steel, leather, or whisky. Everything physical simply represents energy vibrating at a rate we can detect with our five senses.

Yet this concept seems strange to us. We have developed such faith in our five senses to detect the physical world around us that we have difficulty imagining that our bodies consist of more than just what we can see and feel. But in a very real sense, the physical world is an illusion *created* by our senses.

Consider for a moment one of the metal beams holding up a building. It looks solid enough, and our senses of touch and sight tell us that it is solid, as well as strong and heavy. But we also know that this beam is composed entirely of atoms and, furthermore, that each atom is composed of a nucleus of protons and neutrons around which orbits, at ultra-high speed, one or more electrons.

To get a feel for the spatial relationship between the nucleus and the electron, imagine a basketball sitting in the middle of a football stadium. Now imagine an object the size of a golf ball orbiting the basketball at several thousand miles per hour and describing a circle with a diameter as large as the stadium. This gives us a rough picture of the kind of size difference we are talking about between an electron and a nucleus, and the immense space between them.

From this, we can say that an atom is composed of somewhere around 99.99 percent space. Since matter is composed entirely of atoms, matter must be composed of 99.99 percent space. Thus, the aforementioned metal beam is 99.99 percent space. You are 99.99 percent space as well.

The beam looks dense for the same reason that an electric fan when running looks solid. When such a fan is not rotating you can see the spaces between the blades, and you can put your hand through those spaces. When the blades spin very fast, you can no longer see the spaces. And if you try to put your hand between the blades, they will feel like an impenetrable wall. Like a fan's blades, any piece of physical material is made up of a mass of electrons spinning so fast that they appear solid to our senses.

If the electrons in the beam holding up the building were to stop spinning, the beam would disappear in an instant. If all the other electrons around it stopped spinning too, we could imagine the whole building disappearing. No debris would be left, no dust, nothing. To a viewer, it would appear that the building had simply evaporated.

Matter is simply vibration—nothing more, nothing less. Our senses are tuned to these vibrations, and our minds convert them into matter. Sounds weird, but it's true.

**Assumption:** We have subtle bodies as well as physical bodies. The physical body vibrates at the frequency of matter (the World of Humanity), while the highest two of the five subtle bodies vibrate closer to the frequency of the soul (the World of Divine Truth).

Besides the flesh and bone of our physical bodies, we consist of other energy patterns we cannot see or measure. These are called our subtle bodies or subtle fields. They vibrate at frequencies an octave or two higher than those bodies condensed as matter and are beyond the range of our senses and most detection instrumentation. These are:

*The Etheric Body*
The etheric body carries the energetic template of the body. It ensures the continuation of the patterns, harmonies, and disharmonies within the body while the body constantly renews itself. Your body is not the same as it was a year ago, for not one cell exists in your body that is more than one year old.

The etheric body interacts with your genetic code and holds the memory of who you are, the shape of your nose, your height, what prejudices you hold, what you like to eat, your strengths, your weakness, your illness patterns, and so on.

## The Emotional Body

The emotional body vibrates one octave above the etheric field. Also known as the astral body, it suffuses the etheric field and the bioenergetic fields of the physical body and manifests in the body as feelings.

An emotion constitutes a thought attached to a feeling that usually results in a physical response or action. When energy flows freely from the emotional field through the etheric field and the physical body, everything works together beautifully.

When we restrict our emotional energy through suppression or repression, we create energy blocks in both our etheric and emotional fields as well as in our physical body.

The perceptual shift required for forgiveness cannot happen while anger and resentment are maintained in the emotional body. Any energy stuck in the emotional body must be cleared first.

## The Mental Body

This field governs our intellectual functioning and is responsible for memory, rational thinking, concrete thought, and so on. Of course, there are scientists who still maintain that thinking and other mental processing can be explained in terms of brain biochemistry. Suffice it to say that the scientists who follow the logic of quantum physics believe that the mind goes beyond the brain, beyond even the body. They believe that brain and mind interact *holographically* and that each cell contains a blueprint of the whole. Many researchers believe that memory resides in holographic form in an energetic field that exists beyond the body.

Proof of this is continually showing up as a by-product of organ replacement surgery. One celebrated story concerns a person who received a liver transplant. Some months after the operation, he began having a recurring dream that did not make sense to him. After some investigation, he discovered that the person who had donated the liver had dreamed the same dream for many years. The memory of that dream was apparently embedded in the cellular structure of the liver.

### The Causal Body or Intuitional Field

At the next octave up lies the body we might call our soul, our Higher Self, or our connection to the World of Divine Truth. Also called the causal body, this one provides our bridge to the spiritual realm. Whereas the mental field deals with ideas and thought forms at the concrete level, this field deals with them at the conceptual, abstract, iconic, and symbolic level. It deals with essence, intuition, and "direct knowing." The causal body extends beyond the individual and penetrates the collective mind—or what Jung called the collective unconscious, a single mind to which we all individually connect and have access.

The idea of subtle bodies rising in harmonics is by no means new; it has been included in many great spiritual traditions throughout the whole world, especially those of the East.

**Assumption:** Universal energy as life force and consciousness is brought into our body via the chakra system. The first three chakras are aligned with the World of Humanity while the fourth through eighth align more closely with the World of Divine Truth.

In addition to the ocean of energy containing our differently vibrating subtle bodies, we human beings possess a system of energy centers that align vertically in our bodies. These are known as chakras—"wheel" in Sanskrit, because they are like vortices of spinning energy.

The chakras act like transformers. They take the energy or life force (prana, chi, Christ energy) that comes to us from the universe and step it down to frequencies that can be used by the biomolecular and cellular processes of the physical body. The chakras also represent the locations where each of the subtle bodies link to the physical body, thus bringing different levels of consciousness into our being. They process our daily

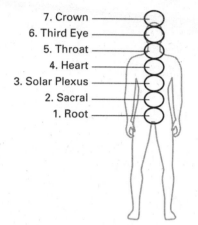

7. Crown
6. Third Eye
5. Throat
4. Heart
3. Solar Plexus
2. Sacral
1. Root

FIGURE 13   **The Human Chakra System**

experiences, thoughts, and feelings while also carrying long-term data relating to personal and tribal history, long-established thought patterns, and archetypes.

The first three chakras possess levels of consciousness vibrating at the lower frequencies of the existential chain and rooted in the World of Humanity. They carry the energy of the victim archetype. Traditional forgiveness is the only type of forgiveness possible with the consciousness of the first three chakras. The consciousness that comes through the fifth, sixth, seventh, and eighth chakras is more likely to align with energies from the World of Divine Truth, while the fourth, the heart chakra, provides the link between the World of Humanity and the World of Divine Truth.

205

In addition, each chakra is associated with an endocrine gland and corresponds to a particular nerve nexus in the same area. Each also has a color and sound associated with it, and each nourishes a particular part of the body. Chakras also serve as information databanks and processors associated with the parts of the body to which they are attached and the functions they serve.

- The first (root) chakra carries data relating to being grounded to Mother Earth and issues of basic trust, security, and the will to live. This chakra runs on tribal/social consciousness.

- The second (sacral) chakra carries data relating to creativity, sexual energy, money, and guilt. This chakra, like the first, runs on tribal/social consciousness.

- The third (solar plexus) chakra carries data relating to power and control, social and familial relationships, betrayal, and anger. This chakra is also directed by tribal/social consciousness.

- The fourth (heart) chakra carries data about matters of the heart, relationships, love, nurturing, and compassion. This is the first chakra to energize individuality and self-determination independent of social group consciousness.

- The fifth (throat) chakra carries data about things expressed or withheld in matters of personal power, individual will, and creative expression. It is directed by individual as opposed to group consciousness.

- The sixth (third eye) chakra carries data relative to intuitive knowledge, clairvoyance, and the will to know the truth. In this case, truth refers to knowing not defined by group consciousness, but directly from individual experience of cosmic consciousness.

- The seventh (crown) chakra carries data about spiritual awareness and connection to Source.

- The eighth chakra, which lies above the head, represents our contract or agreement for incarnation and contains our life's mission.

Though central to Eastern medical traditions, the chakra system gets zero attention from Western medical science, and there generally exists very little recognition in the West of its central importance to our health, spiritual well-being, and vibratory rate.

In truth, the chakras are crucial. When these energy centers become out of balance—as they do when we become emotionally upset or traumatized, for instance—they reverse rotation, become very erratic, and in some cases close down almost entirely. Anger, resentment, and hurt will tend to close the heart and throat chakras, guilt and lack of trust will weaken the sacral chakra, and so on. The effects of such energy imbalances will be felt as lethargy, a general malaise, low sex drive, inability to speak our truth, and a whole host of symptoms for which a medical cause cannot be found. If the chakras remain out of balance for a long time, it is inevitable that an effect will indeed, sooner or later, manifest as disease in the physical body. As we noted with the subtle bodies, disease almost always begins in the energy fields—which include the chakras—and moves into the physical body, appearing finally as physical breakdown.

Fortunately, chakras can be restored to balance quite easily. There are practitioners who are sensitive enough to feel the energy of each chakra and have techniques for rebalancing them. Most forms of energy medicine such as acupuncture, homeopathy, aromatherapy, and many others act directly on the chakras and bring them into balance.[4]

# part four

# Tools for
# Radical Forgiveness

# 16  A Spiritual Technology

IN WRITING THE first edition of this book, I had two objectives in mind. First, I wanted to explain the concept of Radical Forgiveness as simply as I could in order to make it accessible to as many people as possible. Second, I wanted to make it as practical as I could so that people could use it in their everyday lives. That meant including tools that were not only effective but quick and easy to use.

As I write this edition, I confess that the extent to which the tools in this book have proven effective more than surprises me. I find myself in awe of how extraordinarily powerful they have proven to be in helping people heal their lives.

I have also come to realize that they work in a way not dissimilar to how homeopathic remedies work. That is to say they work holo-energetically (using the energy of the whole).

In a holographic universe, each minute part of the universe is not only connected energetically to the whole, but contains the whole. Therefore, from an energetic standpoint, you cannot change one part without affecting the whole.

Homeopathy uses this principle by making remedies that affect the energy system of the organism in exactly this way. The tiniest part of an active ingredient is put into water and is then diluted many thousands of times to the point where there is no physical trace of the substance left. What does remain, however, is the energetic imprint of the substance, and therein lies the power to heal. When the person takes the remedy, the subtle body registers the imprint and becomes stimulated to move energy in whatever way it needs to in order to heal at all levels.

The same thing happens with these Radical Forgiveness tools. Just as someone might look at the homeopathic remedy and, seeing only water, find great difficulty in imagining that it has the power to heal, so might someone looking at a forgiveness worksheet, for example, be thoroughly skeptical about its ability to change her life.

Yet it works. Thousands of people have used the Radical Forgiveness worksheet (see page 257) or listened to the *Radical Forgiveness* CD (see page 363) or walked the circle in the Radical Forgiveness ceremony (see Further Resources section) and experienced miracles in their lives.

These tools work because each of them is simply the delivery system for the secret ingredient: the energetic imprint of Radical Forgiveness, i.e., the willingness to be open to the idea that there is nothing to forgive.

The process is very subtle. Mind control or making things happen at the gross level through affirmations, visualization techniques, or hypnosis has little relevance to Radical Forgiveness. It does not require a high level of belief or faith, nor do you need to be in a meditative or altered state. All you must do is use a simple tool that asks little of you in the way of intelligence, discipline, or skill. It asks only that you express a tiny amount of willingness—that's all. In this edition of the book, I have even simplified the worksheet so that in some places you only have to check boxes in answer to a few questions. It still works.

Since forgiveness is always a "fake it 'til you make it" proposition, we are indeed fortunate that it needs only that small amount. If you had to wait until you had 100 percent willingness to believe that the situation was perfect, you would never begin the process.

The following story is an example of how this transformation can occur in an instant using one of the Radical Forgiveness tools—interestingly enough, the quickest and simplest of them all: the 13 Steps to Radical Forgiveness.

## DEBI AND THE 13 STEPS

Debi was a studio singer, which means she sang jingles, commercials, radio IDs, and things like that. She was considered to be among the best in the business. In 1999, she came to study with me to become a Radical Forgiveness coach.

At one point during the training, I wanted to teach her how to facilitate the 13 Steps to Radical Forgiveness. It takes no more than seven minutes and involves responding in the affirmative to thirteen very simple questions.

The thirteen questions all relate to our willingness (the secret ingredient) to see the perfection in the situation whether we understand it or not. The answer to each question is yes.

I asked Debi if she had a situation to work with for this process. She thought for a while and then said: "Yes, here's something I've been upset about for a while. I'd almost forgotten. About thirteen years ago, I was in a studio and in came a guy whom I knew reasonably well but was not real close to. We chatted for a while, and eventually he came out with what was really on his mind. He said, 'Debi, I have this great product that's just perfect to market on the radio, and I need you to do an ad for me. The problem is, I don't have money right now, but will you do it as a big favor to me?'

"Well, I finally gave in and agreed to do for seventy-five dollars what I normally charge a lot of money for. I did the ad, and what do you know, it made him a multimillionaire overnight.

"Some time later, when I ran into him, I suggested he might want to send just a little bit of that my way in appreciation of what I had done for him. His response was, 'Debi, we're not in the business of giving money away!'"

This was perfect. She was obviously into her feelings about it—even after thirteen years! This was understandable given the fact that every time she had turned the radio on over the last thirteen years, there was that ad. As you might imagine, it had all the ingredients of a victim story—betrayal, insult, manipulation, withholding, ingratitude, and so on.

So I immediately proceeded to take her through the process. It took no more than the seven minutes, and as always after doing a process like that, we went on to something else without any further discussion. (Talking about it would destroy the energy field created in the process.)

She went out that evening and returned to her hotel at around 11 p.m. She called me at 11:05 in a state of great excitement. She had checked her voicemail messages, and one was from the studio producer who had helped her do that very ad.

The message went like this: "Debi, that commercial you recorded for Mr. X has come up again, and it needs to be re-recorded. But the copyright has expired, so you would earn all the royalties on it this time. Are you interested?"

Well, as you might imagine, I started jumping up and down yelling, "Hey, this stuff really works!" Then Debi said, "But there's more. When we did the 13 Steps, I happened to glance at the clock on the wall, and for some reason I registered the time quite clearly in my mind. It was 3:01 p.m. That message came in at 3:02! One minute later—and I hadn't spoken with him for months!"

Debi's victim story about how she was used, cheated, dishonored, insulted, and rejected had kept the energy stuck for thirteen years. It was not until she was invited to express a minute amount of willingness to see that she had created that story out of her own perception of the situation—and, during the 13 Steps process, reframed it in a way that reflected spiritual truth—that the energy field collapsed. At no point did we "work" on her story. That would only have given it more power and reinforced it. Instead we used the holo-energetic technology of Radical Forgiveness to transform the energy.

It is interesting to look at what might have been happening here. Most people would have agreed with Debi that this man had betrayed, insulted, and dishonored her with his selfish attitude. Yet the very fact that he exhibited this really quite peculiar kind of behavior was a clue that something else was going on beneath the apparent situation.

At the time that event occurred, Debi's self-esteem was very low. Even though she was always being told what a good singer she was, she could never accept it; she would always put herself down. She had an unconscious belief that she wasn't worthy of what she could rightly charge for her talent.

It is a principle of Radical Forgiveness that if you have a limiting belief which prevents you from becoming whole or from achieving your true purpose, your Higher Self will always find a way to acquaint you with your limiting belief so you can heal it. It can't intervene directly, because you have free will. But it can, through the Law of Attraction, bring into your life someone who will act out your belief for you so you can see it for what it is and choose to let it go.

This man resonated with Debi's limiting belief that she was unworthy, not good enough, and undeserving, and he responded to the call. His Higher Self colluded with hers to play this worthiness issue out so that she could see the idea, feel the pain of it, and choose again.

Far from being a villain, then, this man was in fact a healing angel for Debi. At great discomfort to himself—for who would enjoy being a mean-spirited jerk?—he played out Debi's story for her. Unfortunately, she missed the lesson at that time and simply took it as an opportunity to enlarge her "not good enough" story and prove it right.

Thirteen years later she did a simple little process called the 13 Steps to Radical Forgiveness. As a result, she got to see the truth—that he was providing a healing opportunity for her and that he was in fact her healer. Immediately the energy started to move again, and the money flowed almost instantly in her direction. (Money is just energy.)

A few days after Debi returned from the training, she ran into this man. He made a point of coming up to her and saying, "You know, Debi, I never did thank you for what you did for me all those years ago when you did that first ad for me. You gave me a break, and it worked. I really appreciate it. Thank you." He still didn't offer her money, but that doesn't matter. What she got from him was the acknowledgment that she was previously unable to accept. That was the final healing moment.

Since then, Debi has stepped out into her power. She has stopped hiding her talent by doing anonymous studio work and is now out there doing concerts and recording her own CDs. She has even started her own production company. All that old "I'm not good enough" stuff has disappeared completely, and she is living her purpose.

I always tell Debi's story to convince people of the power of these seemingly simple tools and to encourage people to use them, and I am grateful to her for allowing me to do so.

*Note: Once I became aware of the power of the Radical Forgiveness worksheet to create transformation in people, I was curious as to whether it would prove equally effective as an audio experience. To find out, I crafted thirteen questions that were similar to those on the worksheet and recorded them on a CD. After bringing to mind the story and feeling the feelings, the listener simply had to answer "Yes" out loud to every question that followed.*

*I believe that the potency of the Radical Forgiveness process improves when the questions are heard aloud.*

*The oral response is important, because the body feels the resonance of the word "yes" and it goes in deep. Countless numbers of people have attested to its effectiveness. It is not a hypnotic experience, so many people keep it in the car and listen to it while driving.*

To obtain a copy of this CD, called Radical Forgiveness, *see page 363.*

# 17  The Five Stages
## of Radical Forgiveness

NO MATTER WHAT form the technology of Radical Forgiveness takes, whether it be a workshop, the 13 Steps, the Radical Forgiveness worksheet, or the ceremony, each is designed to take you through the five essential stages of Radical Forgiveness. These are:

## 1. TELLING THE STORY
In this step, someone willingly and compassionately listens to us tell our story and honors it as being our truth in the moment. (If you are doing a worksheet, this person might be yourself.)

Having our story heard and witnessed is the first step to letting it go. Just as the first step in releasing victimhood is to own it fully, so must we own our story in its fullness from the point of view of being a victim and avoid any spiritual interpretation at this stage.

Here we must begin from where we are (or were, if we are going back into the past to heal something), so that we can feel some of the pain that caused the energy block in the first place.

## 2. FEELING THE FEELINGS

This is the vital step that many so-called spiritual people want to leave out, thinking that they shouldn't have "negative" feelings. That's denial, pure and simple, and it misses the crucial point that authentic power resides in our capacity to feel our feelings fully and, in that way, show up as fully human. It is only when we give ourselves permission to access our pain that our healing begins. The healing journey is essentially an emotional one. But it doesn't have to be all pain either. It is surprising how, as we go down through the levels of emotion and allow ourselves to feel the authentic pain, it can quickly turn to peace, joy, and thankfulness.

## 3. COLLAPSING THE STORY

This step looks at how our story began and how our interpretations of events led to certain (false) beliefs forming in our minds that have determined how we think about ourselves and how we have lived our lives. When we come to see that these stories are, for the most part, untrue and serve only to keep us stuck in the victim archetype, we become empowered to make the choice to stop giving them our vital life force energy. Once we decide to retrieve our energy, we take back our power, and the stories wither and die.

It is also at this step that we might exercise a high degree of compassion for the person we are forgiving and bring to the table some straightforward, honest-to-goodness understanding of the way life often is and just how imperfect we all are—and the realization that we are all doing the very best we can with what we are given. Much of this we might categorize as traditional forgiveness, but it is nevertheless important as a first step and a reality check. After all, most of our stories have their genesis in early childhood, when we imagined that the whole world revolved around us and that everything was our fault.

So this is where we can give up some of that child-centered woundedness. Here we can bring our adult perspective to bear and confront our inner child with the plain truth of what really did or didn't happen, as distinct from our interpretations about what we think happened. It is amazing how ridiculous many of our stories seem once we allow the light in. But the real value in this step is in releasing our attachment to the story, so we can more easily begin to make the transition required in the next step.

## 4. REFRAMING THE STORY

This is where we allow ourselves to shift our perception in such a way that instead of seeing the situation as a tragedy, we become willing to see that it was in fact exactly what we wanted to experience and was absolutely essential to our growth. In that sense, it was perfect. At times we will be able to see the perfection right away and learn the lesson immediately. Most often, however, it is a matter of giving up the need to figure it out and surrendering to the idea that the gift is contained in the situation, whether we know it or not. It is in that act of surrender that the real lesson of love is learned and the gift received. This is also the step of transformation, for as we begin to become open to seeing the divine perfection in what happened, our victim stories, which were once vehicles for anger, bitterness, and resentment, become transformed into stories of appreciation, gratitude, and loving acceptance.

## 5. INTEGRATION

After we have allowed ourselves to be willing to see the perfection in the situation and turned our stories into ones of gratitude, it is necessary to integrate that change at the cellular level. That means integrating it into the physical, mental, emotional, and spiritual bodies so that it becomes a part of who we are. It's like saving what you have done on the computer to the hard drive. Only then will it become permanent.

In my workshops, I find that Satori Breathwork is a very good way to integrate the change, whether it is done as part of the workshop or soon thereafter. This entails lying down and breathing consciously in a circular fashion to loud music (see Chapter 27).

Using the worksheet method, the integration comes through writing the statements and then reading them out loud. Using the 13 Steps, it comes through making the verbal affirmation to see the perfection. With the ceremony (see Further Resources), the act of walking across the circle and saying something of an affirmative nature to someone else coming in the other direction is what accomplishes integration. Ritual, ceremony, and, of course, music are all used to integrate the shift in perception that is Radical Forgiveness.

These five stages don't necessarily occur in just this order. Very often we move through them, or some of them at least, simultaneously, or we keep coming back and forth from one stage to another in a kind of circular or spiraling fashion.

# 18 Fake It Till You Make It

FORGIVENESS IS A journey, and it always begins from a place of no forgiveness. Getting there can take years or minutes, and we know now that this is a matter of choice. Traditional forgiveness takes a long time, but we can do it quickly through Radical Forgiveness simply by expressing our *willingness* to see the perfection. Each time we do this, it represents an act of faith, a prayer, an offering, a humble request for divine assistance. We do this at moments when we feel unable to forgive, and in that sense it is a fake-it-till-you-make-it process.

## SURRENDERING

Faking it until you make it really means surrendering to the process, neither putting forth effort nor trying to control the results. In the Seattle study mentioned in Chapter 13, the more effort the participants put into trying to forgive, the more difficult they found it to let go of their hurt and anger. After they stopped trying to forgive and control the process, at some point in time forgiveness just happened.

It is true that the energetic shift from anger and blame to forgiveness and responsibility happens much more quickly with Radical Forgiveness, because, using the tools given here, we can drop the victim consciousness. Consciousness, you will recall from Chapter 13, changes time. Nevertheless, even with Radical Forgiveness, we must enter the process with no expectation of when an energy shift might happen—even though we know that it can happen instantaneously. Exactly when the results begin to show up may depend on things we know little about. It might take a while before we begin to really feel unconditional acceptance for the person involved and peace around the situation, which is how we know when forgiveness is complete. It might take many worksheets, for example, to reach this point.

However, it can be of comfort to many to learn that we do not have to like the person to forgive them. Neither do we have to stay in their company if their personality and/or their behavior is toxic to us. Radical Forgiveness is a soul-to-soul interaction and requires only that we become connected at the soul level. When we feel this unconditional love for their soul, our soul joins theirs and we become one.

## TAKING THE OPPORTUNITY

Whenever someone upsets us, we must recognize it as an opportunity to forgive. The person upsetting us may be resonating something in us that we need to heal, and in that case we can choose to see it as a gift—if we care to shift our perception. The situation also may be a replay of an earlier time when someone did something similar to us. If so, this current person represents all the people who have ever done this to us before. As we forgive this person for the current situation, we forgive all others who behaved likewise, as well as forgiving ourselves for what we might have projected onto them.

An example of this appears as a diagram on page 35. Here, Jill's story is represented as a time line on which appear all the opportunities she had been given to heal her original pain arising out of her misperception that she was "not enough." When she finally saw what was happening in the situation with Jeff and forgave him (healed), she automatically forgave and healed every previous occasion—including the original one with her father. Her entire story, including those aspects of it connected to her previous husband, collapsed in an instant as soon as that lightbulb went on.

This is why Radical Forgiveness requires no therapy as such. Not only does forgiving in the moment heal all the other times the same or a similar thing happened—including the original situation—but you don't have to know what the original situation was. That means you don't have to go digging up the past trying to figure out exactly what the original pain was. It is healed anyway, so what's the point?

## FIRST AID FORGIVENESS TOOLS

The following chapters contain processes that shift energy and offer opportunities to change our perception of what might be happening in a given situation. This change constitutes the essence of Radical Forgiveness. All of these processes bring us into the present moment by helping us retrieve our energy from the past and withdraw it from the future, both of which must be done for change to occur. When we are in the present moment, we cannot feel resentment, because resentment only lives in the past. Neither can we feel fear, because fear only exists in relation to the future. We find ourselves, therefore, with the opportunity to be in present time and in the space of love, acceptance, and Radical Forgiveness.

Some of the tools included in this section are more appropriate for use at the very moment when a situation requiring forgiveness occurs. They help to jerk us into an awareness of what may be happening before we get drawn too deeply into a drama and go to

Victimland. When our buttons get pushed, we easily move straight into the defense/attack cycle. Once in this cycle, we find it tough to get out. Using these quick tools helps us to avoid ever beginning the cycle. The Four Steps to Forgiveness process (see Chapter 22, page 303) is one of these. It is easy to remember, and you can say it to yourself in the moment.

Other tools described in the following chapters are designed for use when we are in a more reflective state of mind. The Radical Forgiveness worksheet works wonders in this regard. Use them all as an act of faith in the beginning. The payoff will prove incredible in time. Consistent use of these tools helps us to find a peace we may never have known was even possible.

# 19  Feeling the Pain

FEELING THE FEELINGS is the second stage in the forgiveness process, and it usually arises as a consequence
of telling the story. This step requires that we give ourselves permission to feel the feelings we have around a
given situation—and to feel them fully. If we try to forgive using a purely mental process—thus denying that
we feel angry, sad, or depressed, for example—nothing
happens. I have met many people, especially those who
think of themselves as spiritual, who feel that feelings
are to be denied and given over to Spirit. That's known
as a "spiritual bypass."

In 1994, I agreed to do a workshop in England. This
was ten years after I had immigrated to America, and I
had quite forgotten the extent to which English people
resist feeling their feelings.

The workshop was to take place in a monastery
in the west of England, and, as it happened, most of
the participants were spiritual healers. The workshop

attendees and I arrived at the monastery, but there was no one from the monastery around, so we went in and rearranged the furniture. I began the workshop by explaining that life was essentially an emotional experience for the purpose of our spiritual growth and that the workshop was designed to help us get in touch with emotions we have buried. Well, you would have thought I was telling them they had to dance naked around a fire or something! Here's the essence of what they all said: "Oh, no. We are spiritual. We have transcended our emotions. We don't give our emotions any credence at all. If we have them, we simply ask Spirit to take them away, and we go straight to peace. We don't believe in this kind of work."

About an hour into the workshop, I knew I had a disaster on my hands. It was like swimming through treacle. I couldn't get through at all, and there was no way they were going to do this work. I was feeling progressively more awful every moment and was convinced that the workshop was going to fall apart completely.

At this point Spirit intervened. A young monk in full habit burst into the room demanding to know who was in charge. When I said I was, he demanded that I go outside with him. He wanted to "talk" to me, but I could see that he was seething with anger; he was all red and puffed up. I said that I was conducting a seminar and that I would come and find him when I was finished.

He went out very upset but came back almost immediately, clearly enraged. He pointed his finger at me, hooked it as if to motion me toward him, and screamed, "I want to see you, right now!"

It was the gesture with the finger that got me. All the frustration and tension of the past hour came rushing to the surface. I turned to my class and said in a very menacing tone, "Just watch this!" I strode over to the red-faced, puffed-up monk and told him in no uncertain terms, pointing back at him with my finger very close to his face, "I don't care what you are wearing and what those clothes represent—you don't come into my workshop and hook me out as if I were some little schoolboy who has offended you. I'll come out and talk to you when—and only when—I am ready. In fact, I will be done right at twelve noon. If you have anything to say to me, you'd better be outside in the lobby right at that time. Then we can talk. Now, get out of my room!"

I strode back to my class; to a person, they were sitting there aghast with their mouths gaping. (You don't talk to religious figures like that!) "Right," I said, pointing to each one of them in turn, "I want to know what you are feeling right now, in this moment, and don't give me that B.S. that you have given it to the violet flame and you are feeling peaceful, because it is obvious that you are not. What are you feeling? Get real!"

Well, as you might expect, they were in their feelings big time, and we started to discuss them. With the help of the monk, I had broken through their wall of resistance to acknowledging that humans have feelings and that feelings are okay. I had busted their story. They had been doing the spiritual bypass, and I let them know it.

At noon I went out of the room into the lobby. The monk was there. I went straight up to him and, much to his surprise and consternation, hugged him. "Thank you so much," I said. "You were a healing angel for me today. You were my seminar. You saved the whole thing."

He really didn't know what to say. I don't think he got it either, even when I tried to explain it to him. He had calmed down, though, and it turned out that all he was upset about was that I had not rung the bell to let him know we were there. He had been sitting in his room waiting for the bell to ring, not thinking that we might push open the door and go on in. Can you imagine getting so enraged about such a small thing? Do you think he might have had an abandonment or "not good enough" issue running?

That seven-day retreat became one of the best workshops I have ever done, and that's because the participants got real and became authentic. I took them into their pain, some of which dated back to wartime incidents they had never shared before. They came to realize that the power to heal is in the feelings—not in talking or thinking, not in affirmations, and not even in meditation if it involves shutting out feelings.

Another myth is that there are two kinds of feelings, positive and negative, and that negative ones must be avoided. The truth is that there is no such thing as a negative emotion. Emotions only become "bad" and have a negative effect on us when they are suppressed, denied, or unexpressed. Positive thinking is really just another form of denial.

## We Want the Emotional Experience

As human beings, we are blessed with the capability to feel our emotions. In fact, some say the only reason we have chosen this human experience arises from the fact that this is the only planet carrying the vibration of emotional energy, and we have come here precisely to experience it. Consequently, when we do not allow ourselves to experience the full range of emotions and instead suppress them, our souls create situations in which we are literally forced to feel them. (Have you noticed that people are often given opportunities to feel intense emotions just after having prayed for spiritual growth?)

This means that the whole point of creating an upset may simply lie in our soul's desire to provide an opportunity for us to feel a suppressed emotion. That being the case, simply allowing ourselves to have the feeling may allow the energy to move through us, and the so-called problem to disappear immediately.

But not all situations are dissolved so easily. When we try to cope with a deep-seated issue and a remembrance of what seems an unforgivable transgression, such as sexual abuse, rape, or physical abuse, it takes more than just experiencing our emotions to get to the point where we feel unconditional love for the other person. Feeling the emotion fully is just the first step in faking it until we make it, and it definitely cannot be bypassed.

I am not saying that emotional work will not benefit from insight gained through a shift in perception that might have occurred before the emotions were felt and expressed. It certainly will. But the converse does not hold true; the perceptual shift required for Radical Forgiveness will not happen if the underlying repressed feelings are not released first.

Invariably, when we feel the desire to forgive someone or something, we have at some time felt anger toward them or it. Anger actually exists as a secondary emotion. Beneath anger lies a primary emotional pain, such as hurt pride, shame, frustration, sadness, terror, or fear. Anger represents energy in motion emanating from the suppression of that pain. Not allowing one's anger to flow can be likened to trying to cap a volcano. One day it will blow!

Stages one and two of Radical Forgiveness ask us to get in touch with not only the anger but the underlying emotion as well. This means feeling it—not talking about it, analyzing it, or labeling it, but experiencing it!

## LOVE YOUR ANGER

All too often when people talk about "letting go" of anger or "releasing" anger, they really mean trying to get rid of it. They judge it as wrong and undesirable, even frightening. They do not want to feel it, so they just talk about it and try to process it intellectually, but that does not work. Trying to process emotion through talking about it is just another way to resist feeling it. That's why most talk therapies don't work. *What you resist persists*. Since anger represents energy in motion, resisting it just keeps it stuck within us—until the volcano erupts. Releasing anger actually means freeing the stuck energy of held emotions by allowing them to move freely through the body as feeling. Doing some kind of anger work helps us experience this emotion purposefully and with control.

## Anger Work Moves Energy

What we call anger work is not really about anger. It is simply the process of getting energy that is stuck in the body moving again. It might be more appropriately called energy release work. Whatever we call it, the process can be as simple as screaming into a cushion (so as not to alarm neighbors), yelling in the car, beating cushions, chopping wood, or doing some other explosive physical activity.

Combining physical activity with the use of the voice seems to provide the key to successful energy release work. All too often we block the energy of emotion—whether it be anger, sadness, guilt, or something else—in the throat, so vocal expression should always be a part of the process. We should go into it not with the idea of trying to rid ourselves of the feeling, but with the intention of feeling the intensity of it moving through our body—without thought or judgment. If we truly can surrender to the emotions, we will feel more alive than we have felt in a long while, and we will find that the energy has dissipated.

## If Anger Is Scary

For many of us, the thought of bringing up anger may be too scary even to contemplate, especially if terror lies underneath the anger. The person who did these terrible things to us may still exert a strong influence on our subconscious mind. Under these circumstances, it is not advisable to do anger work alone. Instead, we should work with someone who knows how to support us while we feel both the anger and the terror—someone with whom we feel safe and who has experience in helping people to move through intense emotion. A counselor or psychotherapist of some kind would be a good choice. I also recommend doing Satori Breathwork (see Chapter 27) with a skilled practitioner. This provides a way to release emotion.

## Anger Addiction Warning

A note of caution needs to be sounded here. It becomes all too easy to get addicted to anger. Anger feeds on itself and easily becomes resentment. Resentment relishes going over and over an old hurt, constantly revisiting the pain associated with it, and venting the resultant anger in some form. It becomes a powerful addiction in and of itself.

We must realize that anger that persists serves no useful purpose. Consequently, once the energy of anger has been allowed to flow as feeling, we should use the energy to create a positive outcome. Maybe we need to set a boundary or a condition on future interactions with the person around whom our anger revolves. Perhaps we can make a decision of some kind, such as being willing to feel compassion for the person or forgive him or her. Only when we use anger as the catalyst for positive change, self-empowerment, or forgiveness will we prevent it from becoming an addictive cycle.

# 20 Collapsing the Story

THE STORY IS where the pain resides. It is what we write in Step 1 of the worksheet in the next chapter to complete the sentence, "The situation around which I have an upset is or was . . . "

Since it appears to be the source of all our pain and discomfort, it is worth turning the spotlight on our victim story to see the extent to which it is real and whether holding onto the pain is justified. We might find that there's very little in it that is actually true. We might find that it is just a story we have created to keep us stuck in separation in order to reinforce our belief that we are not all one. It might also be that we have created this story to give us clues about what we might need to heal (forgive) within ourselves so that we can come to the realization that we are indeed all one.

Obviously it is this last possibility to which Radical Forgiveness gives attention, for it is my belief that the very purpose of the story—and of course, the roles of all the players within it—is to highlight and bring to conscious awareness that which needs healing. It is in the dismantling of the story that we find our opportunity to learn the real truth about ourselves and to remember who we really are.

In tracing back the story and how it was formed, we usually discover that a core negative belief arose out of the experience. Such beliefs are unconscious but they nevertheless remain active and, in order to reinforce themselves, tend to create circumstances in the world "out there" that prove the belief correct. This is what happened to Jill (see Chapter 1). Her unconscious core belief was "I'm not good enough for any man," and she lived it out. Once we collapsed the story and she saw that it was not true, she healed the core belief and everything worked out.

These core beliefs usually form when we are very young. When something happens to us, we interpret the experience and give personal meaning to the situation. Then we confuse what really happened with our interpretation of what did. The story we make up based on that mixture of fact and fiction becomes our truth and an operating principle in our lives.

For example, let's say our father leaves home when we are five years old. For us, this event is traumatic and painful, but in our mind that is only the beginning

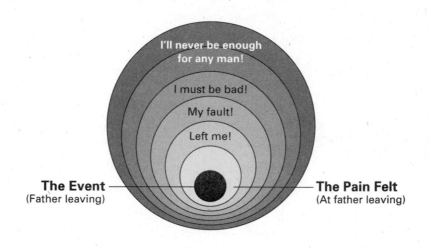

I'll never be enough
for any man!

I must be bad!

My fault!

Left me!

**The Event** ——————————————— **The Pain Felt**
(Father leaving)                                    (At father leaving)

FIGURE 14   **How a False Story Grows**

of our story. At that age we think the world revolves
around us, so we can only see it from that egocentric
point of view. So we make our own interpretations
based on that viewpoint. The first interpretation is
that he left *me!* After that come many more interpretations that expand the story egocentrically, such as:
"It must be my fault. I must have done something to
drive him away. He doesn't love me anymore. Maybe
he never did. I must be a very unlovable person if my
father would leave me. He can't care about me, and

247

if he doesn't care about me, who will? I guess if he doesn't love me, nobody will love me, and even if they do they are sure to leave me after five years because that's the way things are with men who say they love you. You can't really trust men who say they love you because they are bound to leave after five years anyway. I am just not very lovable. I will never have a relationship that will last more than five years. If I was not good enough for my father, I will never be good enough for anyone."

We might also, if we are female—and as happened with a woman in my workshop recently who had this story running—make it up that men are always subject to being "stolen" by other women. Then we will unconsciously create situations where this happens—in this example, after about five years of being in relationship.

These stories become like internal gyroscopes, with their own frequencies that attract events and people to them so that they get played out according to the beliefs they contain. But, as we can see, the only part of the story that is true is the original event: Father left. That might be perhaps 5 percent of the total story. The rest is simply interpretation—assumptions made by a very immature, frightened mind. That makes the story 95 percent B.S. (Belief System)!

Your Higher Self knows that those ideas are not only B.S. but are highly toxic as well, so while it cannot intervene directly (since Spirit gave us free will), it brings people into your life who will lovingly "act out" parts of your story over and over until you realize that it is not true.

Again, this is what happened with my sister, Jill. When our father demonstrated the kind of love for my daughter Lorraine that Jill had always wanted to feel from him and had not felt, Jill took that to mean that she was inherently unlovable. That became the story she believed until she brought someone into her life (Jeff) who was able to make her discover her story and to see that it was false.

### Jesse's Story

Sometimes you are aware of the story, sometimes not. Jesse was at one of my workshops and appeared fully aware of her story but nevertheless did not see the error in it. This was in spite of the fact that she was spiritually very aware. She told us that she had just been fired from her job. "That's okay," she said. "It's my abandonment issue playing itself out again. I get fired or lose a relationship every couple of years. It's because I was abandoned when I was a baby."

I suspected a B.S. story, so I began to investigate the abandonment. What we soon discovered was that

249

her father had died just before she was born and that her mother had become ill and unable to cope when Jesse was about two years old. Consequently, Jesse was reared for a while by her grandparents.

Though she was no doubt traumatized by being separated from her mother, the actual truth of the matter was that her parents never did abandon her—they were simply absent through no fault of their own. To abandon someone is to make a calculated and conscious choice to leave them. It is a deliberate act. Mere absence does not constitute abandonment.

Taking absence to mean abandonment was an interpretation a small child might easily make, and the importance goes way beyond semantics. Interpreting her parents' absence as abandonment, she went on to make a number of other interpretations such as: "If my parents abandon me, I must be a very unlovable person. No one will ever stay with me for more than two years because, if my mother abandons me after that time, everyone will do exactly that. They won't want me after that. They will realize I am a bad person and will leave. That's how life is."

Jesse had been living out of this particular story for all her fifty-two years. Yet it was founded on a complete misinterpretation of the situation. Once she saw that, and from that point on, she was able to let it go and become free from the need to create abandonment every two years.

Even though she had spiritual awareness, she had consistently failed to realize that in providing instances of abandonment every two years, Spirit was in fact giving her opportunities to wake up and heal a toxic story that was a limitation on her life and a wound to her soul. Doing some Radical Forgiveness worksheets on the person who had last fired her helped her clear all the other times she had been "abandoned" over her fifty-two years and neutralized her original abandonment story.

## THE FORGIVENESS CENTRIFUGE

One tool might have saved Jill and Jesse many years of painful struggle. The forgiveness centrifuge helps us separate *what actually happened* in any given situation from our *interpretation* of what happened. If you own the type of juicer where you put carrots and other things in the top and the juice is separated from the fiber by the centrifugal force of the spinning grater, you know what is meant by the term *centrifuge*. A centrifuge is also used to separate plasma from blood, cream from milk, and so on. A washing machine spinning out the excess water from clothes works in the same manner.

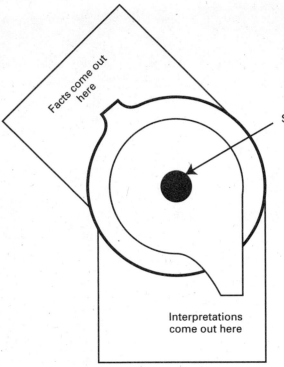

Facts come out here

Story goes in here

Interpretations come out here

FIGURE 15    **Separating Fact from Fiction**

A forgiveness centrifuge simply reverses the process by which we come up with stories about what happened to us. To use it, take the story you are living now—the one that is causing you discomfort. Remember, it is certain to be a hopeless mixture of fact (what happened) and interpretation (all your thoughts, judgments, assessments, assumptions, and beliefs about what happened). Feed the story into the top of the imaginary centrifuge, just as you would with carrots in a juicer, and then, in your mind, see the machine separating the facts from the interpretations.

Then, like any good researcher, first make a list of the facts as they emerge, being as objective as possible. Then make a list of the interpretations you made about the facts.

| # | The Facts About What Happened |
|---|-------------------------------|
|   |                               |
|   |                               |
|   |                               |
|   |                               |
|   |                               |
|   |                               |
|   |                               |
|   |                               |
|   |                               |
|   |                               |
|   |                               |
|   |                               |

Figure 16  **The Facts About What Happened**

After writing down your results, acknowledge the facts and accept them. Recognize that they tell what happened and that no one can do anything to change that. You have no choice but to allow what happened to be exactly what happened, but watch for any tendency to make excuses for what happened—this will impose interpretation on the facts once again. Just stay with what actually took place.

Next, examine every thought, belief, rationalization, idea, or attitude you imposed on what happened, and declare them all to be *untrue*. Affirm that none of them have validity. Tell yourself they just represent mind-talk. Then, recognize how important your ideas, beliefs, and attitudes are to you. On a scale of 1–100, indicate in the left-hand column how much attachment you think you have to each of your interpretations, and then decide which of them you may be ready to drop and which you are not.

## Be Gentle with Yourself

Do not criticize yourself for being attached to any of these ideas, beliefs, or attitudes, or for being unwilling to let them go. You may have had them for a long time. In fact, they may define who you are. For example, if you are an incest survivor or an adult child of an alcoholic, these labels, which represent ideas or beliefs about yourself, may provide a reference for who you are. If you let go of the ideas associated with these labels, you might lose your identity. So, while you want to be firm with yourself in separating what is real from what you have made up, be gentle with yourself and allow time to release these beliefs.

| # | My Interpretations About What Happened |
|---|----------------------------------------|
|   |                                        |
|   |                                        |
|   |                                        |
|   |                                        |
|   |                                        |
|   |                                        |
|   |                                        |
|   |                                        |
|   |                                        |
|   |                                        |
|   |                                        |
|   |                                        |
|   |                                        |

FIGURE 17   **My Interpretations About What Happened**

The next step after this is the Radical Forgiveness reframe—seeing that the story was perfect and had to play out that way. Watch out for the guilt, anger, depression, and criticism you might feel and direct at yourself when you find out you have created your entire life around a set of untrue beliefs. Please, do not do this. Instead, remember that everything has a purpose and God does not make mistakes. Use one or more of the forgiveness tools to work on forgiving yourself and on seeing the perfection in your situation.

If the facts still prove that something "bad" took place—for example, a murder remains a murder no matter what interpretations you may have made—the Radical Forgiveness worksheet provides the best tool to help you shift the energy around that event.

# 21 The Radical Forgiveness Worksheet

THE RADICAL FORGIVENESS worksheet has its origins in one created by Dr. Michael Ryce, a pioneer in the field of forgiveness. He was one of those who, along with my mentor, Arnold Patent, encouraged me to develop Radical Forgiveness.

From the moment I created the Radical Forgiveness worksheet in 1989, using Dr. Ryce's worksheet as my initial inspiration, it has literally changed thousands of people's lives. It is not easy to explain how or why it accomplishes such dramatic results except to say that it helps people to shift their energy. In fact, you could say that doing the worksheet is, in and of itself, an energy experience.

As I have already indicated, all the tools in the Radical Forgiveness tool kit are holographic in nature and require very little in the way of skill, belief, knowledge, or cognitive understanding. All that is required is the willingness to be open to the possibility that there might be a certain perfection in the situation—even if you don't feel like saying it and don't really believe it. The worksheet is simply a way of expressing this willingness to be willing. Your spiritual intelligence picks up on your willingness and makes the connection to Universal intelligence, whatever that is for you. For that reason, I like to think of the worksheet as a form of secular prayer.

Because the worksheet is an energetic instrument that works holographically, it is not subject to the limitations of time and space. That's why the effect is often immediate and distance is never a factor. Doing the worksheet immediately releases the stuck energy in the situation, with the result that everything seems to resolve itself automatically.

Now that you have read this far in the book, you will understand that any time anyone upsets you or triggers negative emotion in you, it's an opportunity to grow. Where before you would have been sucked into the drama, now you can reach for a worksheet, start the forgiveness process immediately, and get results fast.

Sometimes one worksheet is enough, but if the energy is very stuck, it might take many more. It's difficult to tell. Just keep doing worksheets until the energy around the situation, person, or incident dissipates. This could take days or even months.

You will know when you have reached a place of forgiveness by how you feel. If you find yourself simply feeling neutral when meeting the person again, speaking to them on the phone, or even thinking about them, you are probably 90 percent there with little or no charge left around the person or the situation. You are 100 percent there when you can feel nothing but love for that person.

The worksheet on page 292 can be enlarged and photocopied, but you might prefer to download a letter-size one from soundstrue.com/radicalforgiveness.

It helps when completing the worksheet to have a reasonable grasp of the principles underlying Radical Forgiveness, and the following notes serve as a reminder of them. By way of example, answers are filled in as if Jill had completed it at the time she was going through the situation with Jeff as portrayed in Chapter 1.

When we begin working with Radical Forgiveness, we have a tendency to want to do too many worksheets on too many people from our forgiveness list, and to focus on the major issues of the past. But one of Radical Forgiveness's best characteristics lies in the fact that we do not have to dig up the past to heal the big wounds of yesteryear. Whoever is upsetting you *right now* is the person who represents *all* the people who have ever upset you for the same reason in the past. So work with that person first, even if you're thinking that it's no big deal. If it's upsetting you, it *is* a big deal. It could easily lead you to what really matters.

Another misconception is that Radical Forgiveness is just for dealing with the past. It is perfect for that, of course, but it becomes profoundly life-changing when you use it on a more or less daily basis. As soon as an issue arises, the idea is to use this worksheet, or one of the other tools in the book, to dissolve the energies attached to it. This prevents it from becoming a bigger issue, and the situation automatically takes care of itself. And since there must have been a purpose for that issue to have come up when it did, by moving through it using Radical Forgiveness you are healing something.

Another misconception is that a small upset is not important, and therefore not worthy of a worksheet. Nothing could be further from the truth, especially if you have a disproportionate emotional reaction to the situation or event. That's because the small event is triggering a larger amount of energy stuck around a much bigger and unresolved event from the past. The (self-created) small event is a golden opportunity to resolve that old issue, even if you have no idea what it is. You just do the worksheet on the small event until the upset goes away. In this way, you automatically take care of the older issue. The more worksheets you do on a daily basis, the more you clear your energy field of old emotional baggage.

You might want to date and number these sheets and then file them. This allows you to review them from time to time and evaluate the extent to which your consciousness has changed. Alternatively, you might want to do a ritual burning of them as part of the process.

## THE RADICAL FORGIVENESS WORKSHEET
*An Instrument for the True Transformation*
*of a Grievance*

Following is a sample filled-in worksheet and instructions for each step.

**Date:** *8/7/09*    Worksheet #: *3*
**Subject:** *Jeff*    Whomever you are upset about.

**Instructions:** Identify the person, situation, or object about which you feel upset. Do not use the Radical Forgiveness worksheet for forgiving yourself. There is a separate worksheet for this entitled Radical Self-Forgiveness and Self-Acceptance (see Further Resources). The one exception to this is when you are forgiving a part of your body that has let you down by becoming sick or otherwise not functioning correctly. In this case, externalize it by giving it a name other than your own, and speak of it as if it were someone "out there" separate from yourself.

## I.  TELLING THE STORY

1.  The situation around which I have an upset is or was . . . *(Tell the story totally from your victim standpoint, i.e., old paradigm. Use additional paper if necessary.)*

262

*Jeff is abandoning me by focusing all his attention and love on his daughter Lorraine—completely ignoring me. He makes me wrong and accuses me of being mentally unbalanced. He makes me feel worthless and stupid. Our marriage is over, and it's all his fault. He is forcing me to leave him.*

**Instructions:** Be sure to write about the person or object upsetting you in the third person. In other words, tell your story as if you were telling someone else what happened or is happening. Tell the story about your upset from the victim's standpoint. (Victim consciousness is the old paradigm.) Don't hold back. Describe what the situation is or was and how it feels for you right now, and/or what it felt like at the time. Do not edit or overlay it with any spiritual or psychological interpretation. You must honor where you are now, even if you know that you are in Victimland and therefore in the illusion. (Remember, we are never upset for the reason we think.) Knowing that you are experiencing illusion and need to experience it represents the first step toward escaping from it.

Even if we have already awakened to the truth (the new paradigm), we can easily be knocked off balance and perceive ourselves as victims again very easily. Being human requires that experience. We cannot always be joyful and peaceful and see the perfection in absolutely every situation.

2a. **Confronting X:** I am upset with you, *Jeff,*
because . . .
*You have ruined our marriage. You have hurt me and rejected me. Your behavior stinks, and I am going to leave you, you bastard!*

**Instructions:** Be as confrontational as possible with X, and lay out exactly what you blame him/her/it for. This section's small space only allows a few words, but let the words you choose represent the totality of your upset. If the object or situation has no name, give it one, or at least write about it as if it were a person. If the person is dead, speak to him or her as if he or she were there in front of you. If you want to write it out in full, do so in the form of a letter. (See Chapter 24.) This step allows you to address the person directly. However, keep to one issue. Do not discuss other things in the letter or on this worksheet. Reaching your objective—Radical Forgiveness—requires you to get clarity on precisely what you feel so upset about *now*.

2b. Because of what you did (are doing), **I feel:**
*(Identify your real emotions here.)*

*Hurt, abandonment, betrayal, aloneness, sadness, and anger.*

**Instructions:** It is vitally important that you allow yourself to feel your feelings. Do not censor them or "stuff" them. Remember, we came into the physical realm to experience emotion—the essence of being human. All emotions are good, except when we suppress them. Stuffing emotion creates potentially harmful energy blocks in our bodies.

Make sure the emotions you identify represent real emotions you actually feel, not just thoughts about how you feel. Are you mad, glad, sad, or afraid? If you cannot be specific, that is okay. Some people find themselves unable to differentiate one feeling from another. If that holds true for you, just notice what general emotional quality you can feel around the situation.

If you would like to feel your emotions more clearly or strongly, pick up a tennis racket or a bat and beat the heck out of some cushions or pillows. Use something that will make a noise when you hit the cushions. If anger scares you, have someone with you when you do this exercise. That person should encourage and support you in feeling your anger (or any other emotion) and make it safe to do so. Screaming into a cushion also helps to release feelings. As I have stressed many times, the more you allow yourself to feel the hurt, sadness, or fear that may lie beneath your anger, the better.

## II.  FEELING THE FEELINGS
### *Acknowledging My Own Humanness*
3.  I lovingly recognize and accept my feelings and judge them no more. I am entitled to my feelings.

**Instructions:** This important step provides you with an opportunity to allow yourself some freedom from the belief that feelings like anger, vengefulness, jealousy, envy, and even sadness are bad and should be denied. No matter what they are, you need to feel your emotions in exactly the way they occur for you, for they are an expression of your true self. Your soul wants you to feel them fully. Know they are perfect and quit judging yourself for having them.

Try the following three-step process for integrating and accepting your feelings:

Step 1. Feel the feeling fully, and then identify it as either mad, glad, sad, or afraid.

Step 2. Embrace the feelings in your heart just the way they are. Love them. Accept them. Love them as part of yourself. Let them be perfect. You cannot move into the joy vibration without first accepting your feelings and making peace with them. Say this affirmation: "I ask for support in feeling love for each of my emotions just the way it is, as I embrace it within my heart and accept it lovingly as part of myself."

Step 3. Now feel love for yourself for having these feelings and know you have chosen to feel them as a way of moving your energy toward healing.

4. I own my feelings. No one can make me feel anything. My feelings are a reflection of how I see the situation.

Instructions: This statement reminds us that no one can make us feel anything. Our emotions are our own. As we feel, recognize, accept, and love our emotions unconditionally as part of ourselves, we become entirely free to hold on to them or let them go. This realization empowers us by helping us realize that the problem resides not "out there" but in here, within ourselves. This realization also represents our first step away from the victim archetype vibration. When we think that other people, or even situations, make us mad, glad, sad, or afraid, we give them all our power.

5. My discomfort was my signal that I was withholding love from myself and *Jeff* by judging, holding expectations, wanting *Jeff* to change, and seeing *Jeff* as less than perfect.
*(List the judgments, expectations, and behaviors that indicate that you were wanting him/her/them to change.)*

*I made it up that because Jeff was giving Lorraine a lot of attention, he didn't love me. I felt ignored and belittled. I wanted him to put me first. I needed him to make me feel "enough." I judged him as insensitive and cruel. I was judging him and making him responsible for my happiness and requiring him to be different from the way he was. I was not recognizing the truth—that I am loved by him.*

**Instructions:** When we feel disconnected from someone, we cannot love them. When we judge a person (or ourselves) and make them wrong, we withhold love. Even when we make them right, we are withholding love, because we make our love conditional upon their right-ness continuing.

Any attempt to change someone involves a with-drawal of love, because wanting them to change implies that they are wrong and need to change in some way. Furthermore, we may even do harm in encouraging them to change, for though we may act with the best intentions, we may interfere with their spiritual lesson, mission, and advancement.

This is more subtle than we realize. For instance, if we send unsolicited healing energy to someone because they are sick, we are in effect making a judg-ment that they are not okay as they are and should not be sick. Who are we to make that decision? Being sick may be the very experience they need for their spiritual growth. Naturally, if they request a healing, it becomes a different matter entirely, and you do all you can in response to their request. Nevertheless, you still see them as perfect.

So make a note in this box of all the ways in which you want the person you are forgiving to be different or in what respects you want them to change. What subtle judgments do you make about the person that indi-cate your inability to accept them just the way they are? What behavior do you exhibit that shows you to be in judgment of them? You may be quite surprised to find that your well-intentioned desire for them to be different "for their own benefit" was really just a judgment on your part.

If the truth be known, it is precisely your judgment that creates the person's resistance to changing. Once you let go of the judgment, the person will probably change. Ironic, isn't it? (Note: Look to see how many of these judgments and expectations you are making about yourself. This is another way of saying that what you see in another person is what you despise in yourself. Try doing that. It is very revealing.)

## III. COLLAPSING THE STORY

6.  I now realize that in order to feel the experience more deeply, my soul has encouraged me to create a bigger story out of the event or situation than it actually seemed to warrant, considering just the facts. This purpose having been served, I can now release the energy surrounding my story by separating the facts from the interpretations I have made up about it. *(List the main interpretations and circle the level of emotion and attachment you have around each interpretation now.)*

    *I interpreted his caring for his daughter Lorraine to mean that she was more important than me in his*

*eyes. I went from there to interpreting that he did*
*not love me and that I was not enough for him and*
*that he was like all men.*
Level of emotion now:
☐High ☐Medium ☐Low ☐Zero

**Instructions:** This step, in which you list your interpretations of the event, recognizes that most of the pain and suffering we are experiencing is the result of having magnified the situation in our mind and added a tremendous amount of meaning and interpretation to the facts of what actually happened. This is by design, because our higher self wants us to milk the situation for as much separation angst as possible in order to get the most learning and growth from it. But now that we are becoming open to the idea that the situation happened *for* us rather than *to* us, and that it was self-created and purposeful, we can reduce the amount of emotional charge we experience with this situation by simply separating the facts from the interpretations.

When you have noted your interpretations, assess how much charge remains by circling the appropriate level of emotion.

7.  Core negative beliefs I either made up from my story or which drove the story. *(Check those that apply.)*

- ☑ I will never be enough.
- ☐ It is not safe to be me.
- ☐ I am always last or left out.
- ☑ People always abandon me.
- ☐ It is not safe to speak out.
- ☐ I should have been a boy/girl.
- ☐ No matter how hard I try, it's never enough.
- ☐ Life's not fair.
- ☐ It is not good to be powerful/successful/ rich/outgoing.
- ☑ I am unworthy.
- ☑ I don't deserve.
- ☐ I must obey or suffer.
- ☑ Others are more important than me.
- ☐ I am alone.
- ☑ No one will love me.
- ☑ I am unlovable.
- ☑ No one is there for me.
- ☐ Other _____.

**Instructions:** This step recognizes that we nearly always take things personally, especially when we are very young. As children, we are naturally egocentric. When something happens and we attach a meaning to it relating to ourselves, such as "It was my fault," it is only a short step to our forming a core negative belief based on that idea. Look at the interpretations listed in the previous section and see which of the core negative beliefs in your self-concept arise from those interpretations. Many of your dramas may be driven by these beliefs, especially ones like "I'm not good enough." Jill's story was certainly driven by that belief. Again, these beliefs create incredible opportunities for us to experience separation, but now that we have awakened to the truth, we can release them for the falsehoods they really are.

### Now Opening to a Reframe

8. I now realize that my soul encouraged me to
   form these beliefs in order to magnify my sense
   of separation so I could feel it more deeply for my
   spiritual growth. As I now begin to remember the
   truth of who I am, I give myself permission to let
   them go, and I now send love and gratitude to
   myself and *Jeff* for creating this growth experience.

**Instructions:** This is self-explanatory, but as we now get close to the reframe that Radical Forgiveness demands, the process gets more challenging. Sending love and gratitude to one's victimizer is not easy. Fortunately Radical Forgiveness is a fake-it-till-you-make-it process, so just pretend to send love and gratitude if you have to. The process works anyway, so don't worry.

*Noticing a Pattern and Seeing the Perfection in It*

9. I recognize that my Spiritual Intelligence has
created stories in the past that are similar in
circumstance and feeling to this one in order to
magnify the emotional experience of separation
that my soul wanted. I am seeing this as evidence
that, even though I don't know why or how, my
soul has created this particular situation, too, in
order that I learn and grow. *(List similar stories
and feeling experiences (as in 2b) and note the
common elements in them.)*

*I have a longstanding pattern of attracting men
who will not love me the way I want to be loved,
and they always find ways to show me that I am
not enough. Jeff was in a long line of such men.
However, it was odd that he should act so cruelly,
since he is ordinarily such a kind and sensitive
man and hates to hurt people. It was also an
oddity that both girls had the same name—
Lorraine. It was a synchronicity that John was
on a trip from Australia and was going on
to Atlanta to see Colin, which meant I could
tag along whereas I never would have done
it on my own. The timing could not have
been better.*

**Instructions:** This step recognizes that we are curious human beings and that we have an insatiable need to know why things happen as they do. So although I have said elsewhere that we must abandon our need to know, this step offers us the chance to have some fun looking for some of the more obvious clues that would offer evidence that the situation was always perfect in some unexplainable way. So long as we do not make having such evidence a prerequisite for accepting that this was so, there is no harm in it, and it may turn on some light bulbs. Bear in mind, too, that there may well be nothing that strikes you as evidence one way or the other. If nothing stands out, don't worry. It does not mean that the statement is any less true.

The kinds of clues to look out for might be as follows:

- Repeating Patterns: This is the most obvious one. Marrying the same kind of person over and over again is an example. Picking life partners who are just like your mother or father is another. The same kind of event happening over and over is a clear signal. People doing the same kinds of things to you, like letting you down or never listening to you, is another clue that you have an issue to work through in that area.

- Number Patterns: Not only do we do things repetitively, but we often do so in ways that have a numerical significance. We may lose our job every two years, fail in relationships every nine years, always create relationships in threes, get sick at the same age as our parents, find the same number turning up in everything we do, and so on. It is very helpful to construct a time line like the one I did for Jill (see page 35), except that you might fill in all the dates and note all intervals of time between certain events. You might well find a meaningful time correlation in what is happening.

- Body Clues: Your body gives you clues all the time. Are you always having problems on one side of your body, or in areas that correlate to particular chakras and the issues contained therein? Books by Caroline Myss, Louise Hay, and many others will help you to find meaning in what is happening to your body and what the healing message is. In our work with cancer patients, for example, the cancer always turned out to be a loving invitation to change or to be willing to feel and heal repressed emotional pain.

- Coincidences and Oddities: This is a rich field for clues. Anytime anything strikes you as odd or out of character, not quite as you'd expect, or way beyond chance probability, you know you are onto something. For example, in Jill's story, not only was it odd that both girls who were getting the love Jill felt was denied her were called Lorraine, which is not a common name in England; they were also both blonde, blue-eyed, and the first-born of three. Jeff's behavior was also extremely uncharacteristic. Far from being cruel and insensitive, he is an exceedingly kind, nurturing, and sensitive man. I can't imagine Jeff being cruel to anyone or anything. His behavior toward Jill certainly struck me as odd in the extreme.

  Where once we thought things happened by chance and were just coincidences, we are now willing to think that it is our spiritual intelligence making things happen synchronistically for our highest good. It is these synchronicities that lie embedded in our stories, and once we see them as such, we then become free to feel the truth in the statement: "My soul has created this situation in order that I learn and grow."

That last sentence in Step 9 is probably the most important statement on the worksheet. It reinforces the notion that thoughts, feelings, and beliefs create our experiences, and that, furthermore, we order our reality in such a way as to support our spiritual growth. When we open ourselves to this truth, the problem almost always disappears. That's because there are no problems, only misperceptions.

The statement also challenges us to accept the possibility that the situation may be purposeful and to let go of the need to know the how and the why of it. This is where most intellectually inclined people have the greatest difficulty. They want proof before they believe anything. Therefore they make "knowing why" a condition for accepting the situation as a healing opportunity.

It's no good asking why things happen as they do, because this is asking to know the mind of God. At our current level of spiritual development, we cannot possibly know the mind of God. We must give up our need to know why (which is a victim's question anyway), and surrender to the idea that God does not make mistakes, and therefore everything is in divine order.

The importance of this step comes in its ability to help you feel your way out of the victim mode into the possibility that the person, object, or situation with whom you have the issue reflects precisely that part of yourself that you have rejected and which cries out to be accepted. It acknowledges that the divine essence within, the knowing part of yourself, your soul—whatever you want to call it— has set the situation up for you so that you can learn, grow, and heal a misperception or a false belief.

This step also creates self-empowerment. Once we realize we have created a situation, we have the power to change it. We can choose to see ourselves as the victim of circumstance, or we can choose to see our circumstance as an opportunity to learn, grow, and have our lives be the way we want.

Do not judge yourself for creating a situation. Remember, the divine part of yourself created it. If you judge the divine part of you, you judge God. Acknowledge yourself as a wonderful, creative, divine being with the ability to create your own lessons along the spiritual path, lessons that will eventually take you home. Once you are able to do this, you are able to sur- render to the divine essence that you are and trust it to do the rest.

## IV. TOWARD THE REFRAME

10. I now realize that I get upset only when someone resonates in me those parts of me I have disowned, denied, repressed, and then projected onto them.

I see now the truth in the adage, "If you spot it, you've got it!" It's me in the mirror!

**Instructions:** These statements acknowledge that when we get upset with someone, that person is invariably reflecting back to us the very parts of ourselves we most despise and have projected onto them.

If we can open ourselves enough to be willing to accept that this person is offering us a chance to accept and love a part of ourselves that we have condemned, and that he or she is a healing angel in that sense, the work will have been done.

As I have said before, you don't have to like this person. Just recognize them as a mirror, thank their soul by doing this worksheet, and move on. Neither do we need to figure out what parts of ourselves are being mirrored. Usually it is far too complicated anyway. Let it go at that, and don't be drawn into an analysis. It works best without it.

11. *Jeff* is reflecting what I need to love and accept in myself. Thank you *Jeff,* for this gift. I am now willing to take back the projection and own it as a part of my shadow. I love and accept this part of me.

**Instructions:** This statement reminds us that through our stories, which are always full of misperceptions, we create our reality and our lives. We will always draw people to us who will mirror our misperceptions and offer us the opportunity to heal the error and move in the direction of truth.

12. Even though I may not understand it all, I now realize that you and I have both been receiving exactly what we each had subconsciously chosen and were doing a dance with and for each other to bring us to a state of awakened consciousness.

**Instructions:** This statement serves as yet another reminder that we can instantly become aware of our subconscious beliefs if we look at what shows up in our lives. What we have at any particular point in time truly is what we want. We have, at the soul level, chosen our situations and experiences, and our choices are not wrong. This is true for all parties involved in the drama. Remember, there are no villains or victims, just players. Each person in the situation is getting exactly what he or she wants. Everyone is engaged in a healing dance.

13. I now realize that nothing you, *Jeff*, have done is either right or wrong. I am able now to release the need to blame you or anyone else. I release the need

to be right about this, and I am willing to see the perfection in the situation just the way it is.

**Instructions:** This step goes against everything we have ever been taught about being able to distinguish between right and wrong, good and evil. After all, the whole world gets divided up along those lines. Yes, we know that the World of Humanity is really just an illusion, but that doesn't alter the fact that human experiences demand that we make these particular distinctions in our daily lives.

What helps us with this step is realizing that we are only affirming that there is no right or wrong, good or bad, when seeing things from the spiritual big-picture standpoint—from the perspective of the World of Divine Truth. From there we are able to get beyond the evidence of our senses and minds and see divine purpose and meaning in everything. Once we are able to see that, we can also see that there is no right or wrong. It just is.

This step also confronts you with the perfection in the situation and tests your willingness to see this perfection. While it will never be easy to see the perfection or good in something such as child abuse, we can be willing to see the perfection in the situation, be willing to drop the judgment, and be willing to drop the need to be right. While it may always be difficult to recognize that both the abuser and the abused somehow created their situation to learn a lesson at the soul level, and that their mission was to transform the situation on behalf of all abused people, we can nevertheless be willing to entertain this thought.

Obviously, the closer we are to a situation, the more difficult it becomes to see its perfection, but seeing the perfection does not always mean understanding it. We cannot know the reasons why things happen as they do; we must simply have faith that they are happening perfectly and for the highest good of all.

Observe your strong need to be right. We possess an enormous investment in being right, and we learned at an early age to fight to be right, which usually means proving that someone else is wrong. We even measure our self-worth by how often we are right; thus it is no wonder that we have such trouble accepting that something just is—that it is inherently neither right nor wrong. If you really cannot at this point drop your judgment about something that seems awful, just reconnect with your feelings (see Step 3 above), move into them, and admit to yourself that you cannot yet take this step. Still, be willing to drop your judgment. Willingness always remains the key. It creates the energetic imprint of Radical Forgiveness. As the energy shifts, all else follows.

14. I am willing to see that, for whatever reason, my mission or "soul contract" included having experiences like this and that you and I may have agreed to do this dance with and for each other in this lifetime. If it is for the highest good for both of us. I now release you and me from that contract.

**Instructions:** This statement is simply there to remind us of one of the assumptions of Radical Forgiveness: that we come into this life experience with a mission or an agreement with Spirit to do certain things, be a certain way, or transform certain energies. Whatever that mission was or is, we simply know that whatever experiences we are having are part and parcel of the role we came in to play. Princess Diana's story is a great example of that. Please note that the last part of the statement absolves us from the need to know what the mission was.

15. I release from my consciousness all feelings of *(as in 2b):*

**Instructions:** This enables you to affirm that you release the feelings that you had noted in Box 2b. As long as these emotions and thoughts remain in your consciousness, they block your awareness of the misperception that is causing the upset. If you still feel strongly about the situation, you still have an investment in whatever the misperception is—your belief, interpretation, judgment, etc. Do not judge this fact or try to change your investment. Just notice it.

Your emotions about your situation may come back time and time again, and you can make that okay too. Just be willing to feel them and then release them, at least for the moment, so that the light of awareness can shine through you and allow you to see the misperception. Then, once again, you can choose to see the situation differently.

Releasing emotions and their corresponding thoughts serves an important role in the forgiveness process. As long as those thoughts remain operative, they continue to lend energy to our old belief systems, which created the reality we are now trying to transform. Affirming that we release both the feeling and the thoughts attached to them begins the healing process.

## V. REFRAMING THE STORY
### *The Reframe Statement*

16. The story in number 1 was your Victim Story, based in the old paradigm of reality (victim consciousness). Now attempt a different perception of the same event (a reframe) from your new, empowered position, based on the insights you

have experienced as you have proceeded through this worksheet. *(It may simply be a general statement indicating that you just know everything is perfect, or a statement that includes things specific to your situation if, that is, you can actually see what the perfection is. Often you cannot. Be careful not to do a reframe that is based in "world of humanity" terms. Note any positive shift in feeling tone.)*

I now realize . . . *that Jeff was simply mirroring my false belief that I was unlovable, and he was giving me the gift of healing. Jeff loves me so much that he was willing to endure the discomfort of acting it out for me. I now see that I was getting everything I wanted for my own healing and that Jeff was getting what he wanted for his healing. The situation was perfect in that sense and is evidence of Spirit working in my life and that I am loved. Everything is truly in divine order unfolding according to my divine plan. Jeff is a blessing in my life, and I give thanks for him no matter what happens in the future.*

**Instructions:** If you are not able to see a new interpretation that is specific to your situation, that's not a problem. The

Radical Forgiveness reframe might simply be expressed in a very general way, such as, "What happened was simply the unfolding of a divine plan. It was called forth by my own Higher Self for my spiritual growth, and the people involved were doing a healing dance with me, so, in truth, nothing wrong ever happened." Writing something like that would be perfectly adequate. On the other hand, if you did have some insights into how it all worked out in a perfect sense, that would be fine too.

What would not be helpful would be to write an interpretation based on assumptions rooted in the World of Humanity, like giving reasons why it happened or making excuses. You might be exchanging one B.S. story for another, or even shifting into pseudo-forgiveness. A new interpretation of your situation should allow you to feel its perfection from the spiritual standpoint and become open to the gift it offers you. Your reframe should offer a way of looking at your situation that reveals the hand of God or Divine Intelligence working for you and showing you how much It loves you.

**Note:** You may have to complete many worksheets on the same issue before you feel the perfection. Be absolutely truthful with yourself, and always work from your feelings. There are no right answers, no goals, no grades, and no end products here. The value lies in the process, in doing the work. Let whatever comes be perfect, and resist the urge to edit and evaluate what you write. You cannot do it wrong.

## VI. INTEGRATING THE SHIFT

17. I completely forgive myself, *Jill,* and accept myself as a loving, generous, and creative being. I release all need to hold on to emotions and ideas of lack and limitation connected to the past. I withdraw my energy from the past and release all barriers against the love and abundance I know I have in this moment. I create my life and I am empowered to be myself again, to unconditionally love and support myself, just the way I am, in all my power and magnificence.

**Instructions:** The importance of this proclamation cannot be overemphasized. Say it out loud, and let yourself feel it. Let the words resonate within you. Self-judgment is at the root of all our problems, and even when we have removed judgment from others and forgiven them, we continue to judge ourselves. We even judge ourselves for judging ourselves!

18. I now surrender to the Higher Power I think of as *the Universe* and trust in the knowledge that this situation will continue to unfold perfectly and in accordance with divine guidance and spiritual law. I acknowledge

my Oneness and feel myself totally reconnected with my Source. I am restored to my true nature, which is love, and I now restore love to *Jeff*. I close my eyes in order to feel the love that flows in my life and to feel the joy that comes when the love is felt and expressed.

**Instructions:** This represents the final step in the forgiveness process. However, it is not your step to take. You affirm that you are willing to experience it and turn the remainder of the process over to your higher power. Ask that the healing be completed by divine grace and that you and X be restored to your true nature, which is love, and reconnected to your Source, which is also love.

This final step offers you the opportunity to drop the words, the thoughts, and the concepts and to actually feel the love. When you reach the bottom line, only love exists. If you can truly tap into that love, you are home free. You need do nothing else.

So, take a few minutes to meditate on this statement and be open to feeling the love. You may have to try this exercise many times before you feel it, but one day, just when you least expect it, the love and the joy will envelop you.

19. A Note of Appreciation and Gratitude to You *Jeff*.
    Having done this worksheet, *I now see that you did*

*what you did because you loved me enough to push
me out of my victimhood and helped me give up
my belief that I was unlovable. I am grateful to you
and for you being in my life.*

I completely forgive you, *Jeff*, for I now realize
that you did nothing wrong and everything is in
divine order. I bless you for being willing to play
a part in my awakening—thank you—and honor
myself for being willing to play a part in your
awakening. I acknowledge and accept you just the
way you are.

**Instructions:** You began the Radical Forgiveness
worksheet by confronting X. Your energy has probably shifted since you began, even if the shift occurred
only a moment or two ago. How do you feel about
X now? What would you like to say to X? Allow
yourself to write without conscious thought, if possible, and do not judge your words. Let them surprise
even you.

Then, as you acknowledge, accept, and love X
unconditionally just the way he or she is, you recognize
and forgive the projection that made you see X as less
than perfect. You can love X without judgment now,
because you realize that is the only way a person can
be loved. You can love X now, because you realize that

how he or she appears in the world represents the only way he or she can be. That is how Spirit has willed him or her to be for you.

20. A Note to Myself:

*I love myself for having the sense to follow my guidance and go over to America with John so Colin could awaken me to the truth of what was happening, and I love myself for sticking with it.*

I recognize that I am a spiritual being having a spiritual experience in a human body, and I love and support myself in every aspect of my humanness.

**Instructions:** Remember, all forgiveness starts as a lie. You begin the process without forgiveness in your heart, and you fake it until you make it. So honor yourself for doing it, yet be gentle with yourself and let the forgiveness process take as long as you need it to. Be patient with yourself. Acknowledge yourself for the courage it takes simply to attempt to complete the Radical Forgiveness worksheet, for you truly face your demons in the process. Doing this work takes enormous courage, willingness, and faith.

# THE RADICAL FORGIVENESS WORKSHEET
## *An Instrument for the True Transformation of a Grievance*

Date: _____    Worksheet #: _____

Subject: _____

Whomever you are upset with. (*Tip: To fully anchor the transformation, speak everything written here, and what you write, out loud.*)

## I.  TELLING THE STORY

1.  The situation around which I have an upset is or was . . . *(Tell the story totally from your victim standpoint, i.e., old paradigm. Use additional paper if necessary.)*

2a. **Confronting X:** I am upset with you, _____, because . . .

2b. Because of what you did (are doing), I feel: *(Identify your real emotions here.)*

## II. FEELING THE FEELINGS
*Acknowledging My Own Humanness*

3.  I lovingly recognize and accept my feelings and judge them no more. I am entitled to my feelings.
    I feel: ☐ Willing  ☐ Open  ☐ Skeptical  ☐ Unwilling

4.  I own my feelings. No one can make me feel anything. My feelings are a reflection of how I see the situation.
    I feel: ☐ Willing  ☐ Open  ☐ Skeptical  ☐ Unwilling

5.  My discomfort was my signal that I was withholding love from myself and _____ by judging, holding expectations, wanting _____ to change, and seeing _____ as less than perfect.
    *(List the judgments, expectations, and behaviors that indicate that you were wanting him/her/them to change.)*

*(Note: Look to see how many of these judgments and expectations you are making about yourself.)*

## III. COLLAPSING THE STORY

6. I now realize that in order to feel the experience more deeply, my soul has encouraged me to create a bigger story out of the event or situation than it actually seemed to warrant, considering just the facts. This purpose having been served, I can now release the energy surrounding my story by separating the facts from the interpretations I have made up about it. *(List the main interpretations and circle the level of emotion and attachment you have around each interpretation now.)*

| Interpretations I Made Up About the Event | Level of Emotion Now |
|---|---|
| | High   Medium<br>Low   Zero |
| | High   Medium<br>Low   Zero |
| | High   Medium<br>Low   Zero |
| | High   Medium<br>Low   Zero |
| | High   Medium<br>Low   Zero |
| | High   Medium<br>Low   Zero |
| | High   Medium<br>Low   Zero |

7. Core negative beliefs I either made up from my story or which drove the story. *(Check those that apply.)*
   - ☐ I will never be enough.
   - ☐ It is not safe to be me.
   - ☐ I am always last or left out.
   - ☐ People always abandon me.
   - ☐ It is not safe to speak out.
   - ☐ I should have been a boy/girl.
   - ☐ No matter how hard I try, it's never enough.
   - ☐ Life's not fair.
   - ☐ It is not good to be powerful/successful/ rich/outgoing.
   - ☐ I am unworthy.
   - ☐ I don't deserve.
   - ☐ I must obey or suffer.
   - ☐ Others are more important than me.
   - ☐ I am alone.
   - ☐ No one will love me.
   - ☐ I am unlovable.
   - ☐ No one is there for me.
   - ☐ Other _____.

*Now Opening to a Reframe*

8. I now realize that my soul encouraged me to form these beliefs in order to magnify my sense of separation so I could feel it more deeply for my

spiritual growth. As I now begin to remember the truth of who I am, I give myself permission to let them go, and I now send love and gratitude to myself and _____ for creating this growth experience.

I feel: ☐Willing ☐Open ☐Skeptical ☐Unwilling

### Noticing a Pattern and Seeing the Perfection in It

9. I recognize that my Spiritual Intelligence has created stories in the past that are similar in circumstance and feeling to this one in order to magnify the emotional experience of separation that my soul wanted. I am seeing this as evidence that, even though I don't know why or how, my soul has created this particular situation, too, in order that I learn and grow. *(List similar stories and feeling experiences (as in 2b) and note the common elements in them.)*

## IV. TOWARD THE REFRAME

10. I now realize that I get upset only when someone resonates in me those parts of me I have disowned, denied, repressed, and then projected onto them. I see now the truth in the adage, "If you spot it, you've got it!" It's me in the mirror!

I feel: ☐Willing ☐Open ☐Skeptical ☐Unwilling

11. _____ is reflecting what I need to love and accept in myself. Thank you _____ for this gift. I am now willing to take back the projection and own it as a part of my shadow. I love and accept this part of me.
I feel: ☐Willing ☐Open ☐Skeptical ☐Unwilling

12. Even though I may not understand it all, I now realize that you and I have both been receiving exactly what we each had subconsciously chosen and were doing a dance with and for each other to bring us to a state of awakened consciousness.
I feel: ☐Willing ☐Open ☐Skeptical ☐Unwilling

13. I now realize that nothing you, _____, have done is either right or wrong. I am able now to release the need to blame you or anyone else. I release the need to be right about this, and I am *willing* to see the perfection in the situation just the way it is.
I feel: ☐Willing ☐Open ☐Skeptical ☐Unwilling

14. I am willing to see that, for whatever reason, my mission or "soul contract" included having experiences like this and that you and I may have agreed to do this dance with and for each other in

this lifetime. If it is for the highest good for both of us. I now release you and me from that contract.

I feel: ☐Willing ☐Open ☐Skeptical ☐Unwilling

15. I release from my consciousness all feelings of *(as in 2b)*:

## V. REFRAMING THE STORY
### *The Reframe Statement*

16. The story in number 1 was your Victim Story, based in the old paradigm of reality (victim consciousness). Now attempt a different perception of the same event (a reframe) from your new,

empowered position, based on the insights you have experienced as you have proceeded through this worksheet. *(It may simply be a general statement indicating that you just know everything is perfect, or a statement that includes things specific to your situation if, that is, you can actually see what the perfection is. Often you cannot. Be careful not to do a reframe that is based in "world of humanity" terms. Note any positive shift in feeling tone.)* I now realize . . . .

## VI. INTEGRATING THE SHIFT

17. I completely forgive myself, _____, and accept myself as a loving, generous, and creative being. I release all need to hold onto emotions and ideas of lack and limitation connected to the past.

I withdraw my energy from the past and release all barriers against the love and abundance that I know I have in this moment. I create my life and I am empowered to be myself again, to unconditionally love and support myself, just the way I am, in all my power and magnificence.

18. I now surrender to the Higher Power I think of as _____ and trust in the knowledge that this situation will continue to unfold perfectly and in accordance with divine guidance and spiritual law. I acknowledge my Oneness and feel myself totally reconnected with my Source. I am restored to my true nature, which is love, and I now restore love to _____ . I close my eyes in order to feel the love that flows in my life and to feel the joy that comes when the love is felt and expressed.

19. A Note of Appreciation and Gratitude to You _____ . Having done this worksheet, I . . .

I completely forgive you, _____ , for
I now realize that you did nothing wrong and
everything is in divine order. I bless you for being
willing to play a part in my awakening—thank
you—and honor myself for being willing to play a
part in your awakening. I acknowledge and accept
you just the way you are.

20. A Note to Myself:

I recognize that I am a spiritual being having
a spiritual experience in a human body, and I
love and support myself in every aspect of my
humanness.

# 22  Four Steps to Forgiveness

THIS ADAPTATION OF a three-step process taught by Arnold Patent[5] serves as a reminder of our power to attract the events and people we need to feel the emotions we have around a particular issue. The process takes only a few moments, but it is one that literally could save you from getting endlessly caught up in the drama of what is happening and going to Victimland for an extended stay!

When something happens and we get upset, it is extremely easy for us to forget everything we ever knew about Radical Forgiveness. Until these principles become firmly anchored in our minds, whenever our upset creates a lot of emotional turmoil, our tendency is always to default to victim consciousness. The problem is, once there, we tend to hang out there for a very long time. Without a Radical Forgiveness viewpoint, you would will probably stay there for years, which is what most people do, as indicated by the dotted line on the diagram below. But if you know someone who knows Radical Forgiveness and recognizes your symptoms, he or she will have you do a worksheet or listen to the *Radical Forgiveness* CD so you can return to peace. As you will see on the following diagram, each time something happens we default to becoming a victim and go for an extended stay in Victimland. Then we get reminded of how everything might be perfect, so we use the technology to express our willingness to see the perfection and eventually return to a state of peace.

This can be a rough ride, though, and it depends on your having someone who will rescue you. The way to stop the roller coaster is to use the four-step process *before* you have to book yourself a room in Victimland! On the diagram, use of the four-step process is represented by the curves that stop just short of the line at which we usually go unconscious. When we find ourselves using this process naturally, as a matter of course, Radical Forgiveness has become our default lifestyle—one that is, for sure, a whole lot easier!

So, as soon as you find yourself getting upset over something, or even if you find yourself making judgments, feeling self-righteous, or wanting to change something about a situation, use this process to bring your consciousness back into alignment with the principles of Radical Forgiveness.

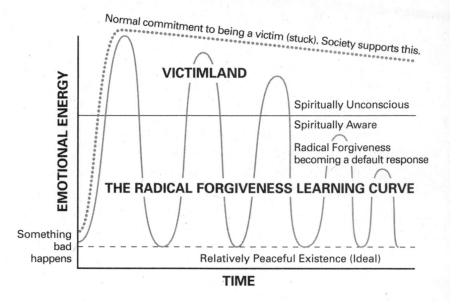

FIGURE 18   **The Victimland Roller Coaster**

## STEP ONE: "LOOK WHAT I CREATED!"

This first step reminds us that we are the creators of our reality. However, we create circumstances for our own healing, so do not assume *guilt* for what happens. Being quick to judge, we often use this step as a way to beat ourselves up. We say, "Look what I have created. Oh, it's terrible—I must be a terrible person, a spiritual failure." Please do not fall into this trap, for if you do, you buy into the illusion.

## STEP TWO: "I NOTICE MY JUDGMENTS AND LOVE MYSELF FOR HAVING THEM."

This step acknowledges that, as humans, we automatically attach a whole string of judgments, interpretations, questions, and beliefs to situations. Our task involves accepting the imperfection of our own humanity and loving ourselves for having these judgments, including the one that says we must be a spiritually moribund person for creating this reality. Our judgments are part of ourselves, so we must love them as we love ourselves. Doing this connects us with what is actually happening in our body and mind and brings us into the present through our feelings. Our energy then shifts quickly and allows us to go to the third and fourth steps of this process.

## STEP THREE: "I AM WILLING TO SEE THE PERFECTION IN THE SITUATION."

The "willingness" step is the essential step in the Radical Forgiveness process. It equates to a prayerful surrendering in the moment to the divine plan and the willingness to love ourselves for not being able to see this plan directly.

## STEP FOUR: "I CHOOSE
## THE POWER OF PEACE."

This fourth step represents a consequence of all the previous steps. By accepting that divine purpose is served in this situation and that what appears to be occurring may be illusory, we choose to feel peace and to use the power of peace in whatever actions are required of us. The power of peace is found when we are fully present in the moment, acting with clarity and focus to do whatever may be required, and being completely aware of our feelings.

Practice this four-step process as often as possible. Make it a part of your awareness. It gives you a way to be in the moment throughout your day.

To help you make this process your practice, it is a good idea to put these four steps on a business-size card for your purse or wallet, or on a 3" x 5" card to keep on your refrigerator.

*Note: The previous printing of this book featured an epilogue on 9/11 that demonstrated the use of the four-step process in such a situation (see Further Resources).*

# 23  Seeing the Christ
## in Another

IF YOU RECOGNIZE that a situation occurring between you and someone else represents an opportunity to heal something in yourself, you can create the healing experience by being in that present moment. A way to bring your energy into present time, as opposed to allowing your mind to be in the past or in the future, requires simply looking at the person with whom you are having an issue and *seeing the Christ in them.*

In this sense, the term "Christ" means the part of them that is divine and one with you and with God. As you do this, you join with them, and in that moment you acknowledge the Christ within yourself. If you have the presence of mind to do this, you will transform the situation immediately.

When we truly join with another person and become one with them, we have no need to attack and defend—so in that moment of joining, we raise our vibration, drop all our mechanisms of defense, and become our true selves. At the same time we let go of our projections and see the other person as a child of God, perfect in every sense. This is the essence of Radical Forgiveness.

## SEEING THE CHRIST IN OURSELVES

It is important to recognize that the mechanism of projection does not just apply to our shadow side. We also project onto other people the things we like about ourselves yet have a hard time acknowledging. Thus we see in those people our own inner beauty, our own creative talent, our own intelligence, and so on.

## THE POSITIVE REFLECTION EXERCISE

This is an exercise taught by Arnold Patent. It is powerful in its effect on everyone who tries it because it asks you to, first, see what is wonderful in another person, and, second, claim that quality as your own. It connects people with their essence—with the Christ in themselves—and allows them to really see who they are. The exercise is usually done in a group setting, but it can be done equally well with two people. It is similar to seeing the Christ in a person, but instead of doing it silently, this exercise is done verbally and with eye contact:

Person A, speaking from the heart, says to Person B, "The beautiful, wonderful qualities that I see in you, that you reflect in me, are . . ." Person B listens and responds by saying, "Thank you." They then switch roles and repeat the exercise.

# 24 Forgiveness Is
## a Three-Letter Word

THIS TOOL SIMPLY involves writing three letters to the person you feel has wronged or hurt you in some way. It works wonderfully when you are really upset about something that has just happened; it even works on something that happened a long time ago.

Vent all your anger in the first letter. Hold nothing back. You can threaten vengeance of the vilest kind if it makes you feel good. Keep writing until you have nothing left to say. The process of writing this letter may cause you to shed a lot of tears—tears of rage, sadness, resentment, and hurt. Let them flow. Have a box of tissues beside you. If you are angry, scream into a pillow or do some physical activity to help you feel your anger. *Under no circumstances mail this letter!*

The next day, write another letter. This one should carry somewhat less anger and vengeance, although it still does not let the person with whom you are angry off the hook for what you believe they have done to you. It should, however, make an effort to bring compassion, understanding, and generosity, as well as the possibility of some sort of forgiveness, into the equation. *Do not mail this letter either.*

The following day, write a third letter. In this one, attempt to describe a new interpretation of the situation based on the principles of Radical Forgiveness. Since this mimics the Radical Forgiveness worksheet, refer to the notes on the worksheet as signposts for your letter, but write it in your own words as best you can (see Chapter 21). This may feel like a struggle at first, but persevere. Remember, you will have to fake it for a while before you make it.

*None of these letters are ever mailed*—it is neither necessary nor desirable to do so. They are designed to shift *your* energy, not the energy of the recipient. Venting your feelings, rather than projecting them once again onto the other person, serves as the objective. Sending the angry letter, in particular, accomplishes nothing whatsoever. Doing so will only keep the attack-defense cycle going, and that will drag you deeper into the drama. Remember, as you shift your energy in the direction of Radical Forgiveness, the energy of the other person changes automatically.

You can either keep the letters for future reference or use them in a forgiveness ritual. My personal preference lies in using the ritual of fire to transform them. Something powerful happens when you see your words turn into ashes and rise up in a column of smoke.

# 25  Forgiveness Rituals

THE POWER OF ritual is underestimated in our society today. When we ritualize any procedure, we make it sacred; thus the ritual speaks directly to our soul. While rituals can be very simple or quite complex, the complexity matters less than the reverence you show the ritual. The ritual invites the participation of the divine in human affairs and, as such, represents another way of praying.

Rituals become all the more powerful when we create them ourselves. When devising your own rituals, be as creative as you can. However, here are some general guidelines and ideas you may want to use.

## RITUAL WITH FIRE

Fire has always been the element of transformation and alchemy. Whenever we offer something up through fire, we tap into primordial beliefs in fire's transformative power. For this reason, a ritual burning of a Radical Forgiveness worksheet, a release letter, or the letter trilogy provides a sense of completion and transformation. Carry out the burning with ceremony and reverence. Say a prayer as the item burns.

Burning scented woods, sage, sweetgrass, and incense will intensify any ritual and bring special significance to a forgiveness ceremony. The smoke from sage and sweetgrass also cleanses your aura, thus removing unwanted energies from your energy field.

## RITUAL WITH WATER

Water possesses healing and cleansing qualities, and we give it the ability to make things holy. Ritualized washing, immersing, and floating can all be used to good effect. For example, instead of burning a release letter, fold it into a boat and let a fast-flowing stream of water take it away.

## BE CREATIVE

Be creative with your rituals, and make them meaningful to you. You may recall the story of Jane, who had brain cancer and had put in the attic a box containing everything associated with a man who broke her heart. I asked her to take the box down from the attic and bring it with her to therapy. Had she not had a seizure and died before we could do so, we would have gone through the box, examining every item in it and what it meant to her. Then we would have disposed of them one by one with a ritual bearing meaning for her. This process would have released much repressed energy.

# 26  Artful Forgiveness

ART PROVIDES A powerful tool for forgiveness and emotional release. One of the most dramatic healings through art I have ever been privileged to witness and/or participate in occurred at the retreat I did in England. One of the participants was a young woman with multiple sclerosis. Her body was weak and wasted, and her voice was hardly audible. Her throat chakra was virtually shut down. She had a husband and two children, but the marriage was basically nonexistent, and she felt trapped, helpless, and hopeless.

At one point during a group art therapy session, she began to draw in a particularly striking fashion. She could not talk, but she kept drawing and drawing. It was hard to discern what she was drawing, but it became clear over time that she was using the medium as a way to regress herself and release old childhood pain.

My wife and I sat there with her as she drew hour after hour, her drawings becoming more and more childlike as time went on. In addition to her pictures, occasionally she would scrawl phrases like "bad girl" and "God doesn't love me" and other words indicating deep shame, guilt, and fear. Finally, she made a crude stick drawing of what she later was able to recall as childhood rape by an uncle. In this cathartic release, she was able to express in drawings what she had found impossible to say in words and sounds. Her throat chakra had shut down because of what she had been forced to do with her mouth. (Her uncle had made her have oral sex with him.) Suddenly, art became an outlet for memories and emotions that had remained repressed for many years. These memories and emotions were responsible for her illness.

To support this woman in her catharsis, my wife went to the far end of the rather large room in which we were holding the retreat. We then asked her to use her voice to tell my wife that she was a good girl, and that God loved her. I made her do it louder and louder until she was shouting at the top of her lungs. After she had shouted "God loves me!" about twenty times, she stopped and looked at me and affirmed, "He really does love me, doesn't he?" That healing moment I will never forget.

Three months after we got back from England, we received a letter from her saying that she had left her husband, gotten a new place to live, and found a job. She was using her voice and asking for what she wanted, and she was finding that she had the power not only to ask but also to receive. She had even started a support group for people with multiple sclerosis and was doing art therapy with them. Her strength was returning day by day, and after three years we still hear from her and marvel at her continuously increasing strength.

If you are not a verbally inclined person and are not comfortable writing things down, try drawing. You may be surprised by what happens when you communicate in this manner. Buy some decent-sized white and black paper as well as some colored pastel chalks and crayons. (The pastels work really well on the black paper.)

Know that to use this tool requires no artistic talent whatsoever: it is not about painting pretty pictures. In fact, if you are full of anger, your pictures will probably be anything but pretty. It is about getting emotions and thoughts out on paper.

Begin drawing with no expectations or preconceived ideas. You might ask God or your spirit guides to help you release through the process of drawing and coloring whatever needs releasing—and then simply start. Whatever wants to come, allow it. Do not judge. Just go with the flow. Do it like a meditation. If you want to tell a story, do that. If you just want to use color, do that. Do whatever you feel like doing.

To use art therapy as a forgiveness tool, use an approach similar to that of the letter trilogy. Do a series of drawings that express how you felt about what a particular person did to you; these pictures would express your anger, fear, pain, sadness, and so on. Then move into a more compassionate and understanding frame of mind and do some drawings that reflect this attitude. Do a third set that expresses the feeling of Radical Forgiveness. You might want to put some time between each phase, or you can do them all in the same sitting. Make sure, however, that once you start doing this art therapy, you complete all three stages—even if you only do three drawings in all. Doing just the first one, for example, might leave you stuck in anger.

As you finish each picture, hang it on a wall. Place the pictures in the precise order in which you complete them, and create a vertical or horizontal band on the wall with them. If you are creating a vertical display, begin with the first of the angry ones at the bottom and end with the last Radical Forgiveness one at the top. When you place them in such a manner, you will be amazed to see the progression and the change in the quality of the energy each picture expresses.

Title each drawing and date it. Spend some time with the drawings. Let them "speak" to you. While you were drawing each picture, you were thinking certain thoughts. When you look at the drawing later, clear your mind of those thoughts and examine the pictures for anything else of importance. Invite others you trust to give you their interpretations of the pictures; they may see things you do not. Ask for their input by saying, "If this were your picture, what would you see?" If what they see resonates with you, fine. If it does not really ring true for you, that is fine too. They see into your drawing through their own subconscious, not yours, but you will find that other people's observations will trigger within you a whole new way of looking at your drawings, and you may have some new insights as a result.

# 27  Satori Breathwork

As we have discussed previously, suppressed or repressed emotions have toxic effects on both our mental and physical health. Releasing these emotions serves as the first step in the Radical Forgiveness process. We can release held emotions most quickly and most effectively by using a process called Satori Breathwork, with the guidance of an experienced teacher. (Satori is a Japanese word meaning "insight" or "awakening.")

Satori Breathwork is usually done lying on your back and involves breathing with full awareness in a circular pattern. In other words, you consciously breathe in a manner that has no pause between the in-breath and the out-breath. Carefully selected music is played rather loudly throughout the process.

The person breathes for forty to sixty minutes through an open mouth, sometimes long and deep into the abdomen and at other times fast and shallow into the upper chest. This oxygenates the body to such an extent that the body releases from its cells suppressed emotion that has crystallized into energy particles within the cells. As these energy particles are released, the person often becomes consciously aware of these old feelings in present time.

The feelings may be expressed as pure emotion, such as sadness, anger, or despair, unattached to any memory associated with them. Conversely, the memory of an event, idea, association, or misperception that caused the emotion to be felt and suppressed in the first place may come sharply into focus. It may even surface in a symbolic way or in the form of a metaphor. For each person and in each breathing session, the experience is different—as well as impossible to predict.

As emotions come up, the person "breathes through" them, which allows the person not only to feel them fully but to release them. We often stop breathing to hold emotions in check, so breathing through them allows this feeling and release to take place. In some cases, the person expresses them verbally and kines-thetically while breathing. No matter how the emotions are released, almost invariably a sense of profound calm and deep peace results from the process.

This simple technique provides dramatic and long-lasting healing effects. I have no hesitation in recommending it to anyone who is serious about wanting to clear out their emotional closet. (See Further Resources for more information.)

The effects of Satori Breathwork are profound precisely because they happen completely within the person, without any interjection, guidance, steering, or manipulation whatsoever by the facilitator. In fact, a facilitator is only present to hold the space as safe and support the breather in moving through the feelings—which sometimes can be scary—rather than suppressing them again. I would not recommend that you do this process on your own for that reason.

Conscious connected breathing is also called rebirthing, because researchers have found that breathwork gives us access to memories and emotions lodged in our cells as early as our *in utero* experience, during the actual birth process, and soon after birth. Birth represents our first major life trauma, and we form profound ideas about struggle, abandonment, safety, and acceptance as we go through this experience. These ideas often become beliefs that literally run our lives. When someone re-experiences their birth and releases the traumas and beliefs they formed at that time, their lives change dramatically.

Another great benefit of Satori Breathwork comes from the fact that it integrates new energy patterns into our existing energy fields and restructures our subtle bodies accordingly. This means that when you shift your perception, have an insight, or release old emotional patterns, breathwork integrates this into your body's data banks. Using the computer analogy, it is as if breathwork serves as a downloading process in which data currently stored in the short-term computer memory is transferred to the hard drive for permanent storage.

This also explains why Satori Breathwork is so important in the Radical Forgiveness process. It accomplishes these tasks, not just at the beginning of the process for the purpose of emotional release, but afterward too, when our belief systems change and all the resulting changes in our energy fields need integrating. The integration process anchors the changes in our bodies and helps prevent us from going back to our old ways.

I would suggest that you have between ten and twenty supervised breathing sessions over a period of time, which may take up to a year. After that, you can probably do the breathing process on your own.

# 28  The Radical Release Letter

THE RELEASE LETTER is an adaptation of a letter given to me by hypnotherapist and mind/body therapist Dr. Sharon Forrest of the Forrest Foundation, a nonprofit corporation dedicated to alternative holistic healing, located in Mexico.

The Release Letter proclaims to your Higher Self and to every part of your being that you give full permission for all aspects of unforgiveness still remaining in any situation to be released. It also serves as an instrument of self-forgiveness, for it recognizes that you have created the experiences as a way to learn and to grow.

Photocopy the letter as written on the following page and enlarge it to an appropriate size. To use the Release Letter, fill in the blanks, have it witnessed by someone, and then burn it in a ritual manner.

Date: _____ Name: _____

Dear Higher Self:

I, _____, hereby grant you, my Higher Self, my Soul, my Super-Conscious Mind, my DNA, my cellular memory, and all parts of myself that might want to hold onto unforgiveness for whatever reason, permission to release all of the misunderstandings, unfounded beliefs, misinterpretations, and misguided emotions, wherever they may reside, whether in my body, my unconscious mind, my DNA, my conscious mind, my subconscious mind, my unconscious mind, my chakras, and even my Soul, and I ask all those who want the best for me to assist in this releasing process.

I, _____, thank you, my Soul, for creating the experiences that created the unforgiveness, and I realize that on some level they have all been my teachers and have offered opportunities for me to learn and grow. I accept the experiences without judgment and do hereby release them to the nothingness from which they came.

I, _____, do hereby forgive _____ .

I release him/her to his/her highest good and set him/her free. I bless him/her for having been willing to be my teacher. I sever all unhealthy attachments to this person and send him/her unconditional love and support.

I, _____, do hereby forgive myself, accept myself just the way I am, and love myself unconditionally just the way I am, in all my power and magnificence.

I, _____, do hereby release myself to my highest good and claim for myself freedom, fulfillment of my dreams, wishes, and goals, clarity, love, full expression, creativity, health, and prosperity.

Signed: _____ Date: _____
Witnessed by: _____ Date: _____

# 29  The Forgiveness Rose

WHEN WE OPEN our hearts to others, we become vulnerable and face the danger of becoming the target for their projections. Their psychic energy can become mixed with ours, and this can deplete our energy.

The more workshops I do, the more I realize that in many cases the problems people appear to be having with someone in particular stem from the fact that the latter person is able to get into and manipulate their energy field. Almost invariably, the one with whom they have the problem seems to be entering through the third chakra, which is the one where issues of power and control are stored. Once in, it is easy for that person to control them—sucking their energy or dumping their own energy onto them at will. Of course, this is all done subconsciously—without awareness and hopefully without malice—but it can be debilitating to the one being manipulated and puts a great strain on the relationship.

You probably won't be surprised to learn that it is most often the person's mother who is doing the invading and controlling—even from the grave, I might add. It might also be the father, or the spouse, or any other person who wants to have some control over the person's life, but most often it is the mother.

The easiest way for you to stop this or prevent it happening with people you come in contact with is to simply place an imaginary rose between you and the other person. It is a surprisingly powerful protective device.

The rose is a symbol of psychic protection in a great many esoteric writings. For whatever reason, it possesses a great deal of potency in this regard, probably because it is the universal symbol for love. Visualizing a rose gives us protection from the projections of others, offering a way to block negative energy without closing our heart to the person. I cannot explain why the rose visualization works so well in this regard; in truth, we can create psychic protection with any kind of visualization, because just doing so creates the intention of self-protection. But the rose has been used for centuries for this purpose and seems to work better than most other symbols.

So, from now on, any time you encounter someone whose energy you don't want mixed with your own, visualize the rose existing at the edge of your aura, or

FIGURE 19  **The Rose**

halfway between yourself and the person. Then notice whether you feel differently while in their presence. You should feel a much greater sense of your own psychic space and identity while at the same time being completely present for the person. You don't have to be in someone's physical presence for them to be able to control your energy, so it is a good idea to put up your rose even while talking on the phone.

337

# 30 A Wake for
## the Inner Child

OUR SPIRITUAL EVOLUTION depends heavily upon our recovery from our worst addiction—our addiction to the victim archetype, which traps us in the past and saps our life energy. The inner child represents nothing but a metaphor for our woundedness and a cutesy form of victim consciousness. Wrapping our victim consciousness in baby clothes does not make it any more acceptable. Invoking our inner child still represents addictive behavior.

Please note that I am not talking about the playful, creative, and life-affirming inner child, such as the one described by Richard Bach,[6] or the part of ourselves that comes forward to inspire and awaken us. I am talking about the whining little brat who lives in the back room of our mind, that unhappy victim who can always be relied upon to blame everyone else for our unhappiness. This is the one we pandered to at all those inner child workshops in the 1980s.

For the sake of our spiritual evolution and our eventual release from the victim archetype, we must bring the inner brat's life lovingly to a close. I therefore propose that you hold a funeral and pronounce him or her dead. If you choose to go ahead with this exercise, you will probably grieve the loss of your inner child, and that is okay. No doubt your inner child has given you solace and comfort in your pain over the years, but now is the time to move on. Radical Forgiveness releases you from the need to hold onto the woundedness, so allow yourself to release your inner child now.

As long as you hold onto your past wounds, Radical Forgiveness remains impossible. Clinging to your inner child only holds you back, because that child represents your past wounds. While you want to move on with your life, you may be surprised to find that your inner child wants to move on too! To release your inner child, try the following meditation.

## THE FUNERAL MEDITATION

Sit comfortably and take three deep breaths, allowing your body to relax as your breath leaves your body. Notice any areas of your body that remain tight. Consciously relax them, knowing that during this meditation your body will continue to relax with every breath you take—and soon you will be profoundly relaxed from head to toe. Now look inside yourself and find the room in which sits the young person who has willingly carried your pain. Find the inner child who holds your memories of being abused, ignored, betrayed, abandoned, unaccepted, or unloved.

As you come upon this little person in that room, notice that he or she is surrounded by lists, ledgers, charts, and scorecards. The walls of the room are covered with people's names, what they did to you, and the punishment you have believed they deserve. In the ledgers, the child keeps a careful tally of all the times someone victimized you and what it cost you. Notice the joylessness of this room. As you look at this young child, realize how sad he or she really feels being locked down there alone with the pain, mired in victim consciousness.

Realizing that it is time for a change, you walk across the room and throw open the windows to let in the sunlight. As it floods into the room, the ink on the charts on the wall starts to fade and the ledger books begin to crumble to dust. The lists tacked to the wall also fall to the ground and dissolve. Look at the little person who has lived in this room for all those years, keeping resentment scores day by day. See his or her broad smile and joyous expression.

"Now I am free to go," the child says.

"Go where?" you ask.

"I'm free to go to the next place. I should have left years ago, but I've been waiting for you to release me from this job."

Suddenly you notice that this person, who was young and childlike such a short while ago, is growing old and becoming wizened and gray-haired right before your eyes. Yet a great peace has replaced his or her sadness.

"Thank you for letting me go," he or she gasps, lying down slowly on a couch.

You say, "I'm sorry it's taken so long to bring light into this room. I'm sorry I've held you back."

"That's quite alright," comes the quiet reply. "It really is okay. Time is just an illusion anyway. Goodbye." With that, the little person dies, looking peaceful and serene.

Lovingly, you wrap the little person in a white cloth and take the body upstairs and out into the light. A horse and buggy wait there, and angels hover nearby, singing softly. All the people who have ever been in your life are waiting to pay their respects. All past hurts are forgiven. Love is everywhere. The bells on the horse and buggy ring softly as the entourage slowly begins its journey to the hill where a grave has been prepared. At the graveside, everyone sings and great joy envelops the group. Your angels are with you and support you as you say your last farewell. See the little person being lowered lovingly and gently into the grave while the celestial choir sings. As a stone is placed onto the grave, you feel a new sense of freedom and love moving through you.

You walk to the bottom of the hill where you find a fast-running stream. You wash your hands and face in the water and see your reflection there. Feel the cleansing water of the stream running through your being, taking with it all the dust and debris from the room where the little person once dwelled. Hear the sound of the water babbling over the rocks. See the sun sparkling on the water, and feel the warmth of the sun on your body. Notice the green of the surrounding fields and the many bright flowers all around you. All is well. Open your eyes whenever you feel ready to do so.

Being without your wounded inner child will feel strange for a while, but you will also begin to notice some positive changes. You will feel lighter, less burdened, more in the moment. Your life energy will increase as you retrieve the energy that was previously spent holding on to the wounds of the inner child.

Be prepared to encounter problems with close friends with whom you previously spent time sharing wounds. They will not like this change in you, for they will see that you no longer give your wounds power. Since they remain committed to their wounds, they may be uncomfortable with you; they may even begin feeling as if you have betrayed them. If you are a member of a support group that thrives on sharing wounds, such as Adult Children of Alcoholics (ACOA) or Incest Survivors, be prepared to disconnect yourself from the group. You will probably find your need to attend group meetings diminishing anyway, but if you are the least bit codependent, you might still feel as if leaving the group is a challenge. Stick to your guns, and do not take personally other people's attempts to disconnect from you or talk of betrayal. These people will come around eventually and probably will want some of what they see you have gained.

# Afterword

TWELVE YEARS AFTER first publishing this book, I have finally caught up with my own thinking about Radical Forgiveness being much larger than a mere process of forgiveness—bigger, in fact, than I ever imagined.

I have known from the beginning that Radical Forgiveness has never been about forgiveness *per se*—at least not as we have traditionally conceived of it. It is indeed an alternative way of forgiving that is quicker and more effective than any other form of forgiveness, but it's something infinitely greater, more all-encompassing, and more revolutionary.

It is nothing less than a mind-blowing idea that shatters our existing ideas of reality and challenges our current worldview. It invites us to engage in a process that is rooted in a fourth-dimensional reality that we don't yet understand. Neither is there much proof of its efficacy, other than the evidence of our own awareness of how significantly changed we become when we engage in it. (If you've done a worksheet, you'll know what I mean.)

It requires that we suspend our normal way of thinking about ourselves and our relationship to the world at large, and be open to the possibility that we can begin operating from this new reality—before we really know what it is or how it works—just by being willing to do it.

But the truly amazing gift that it offers humanity lies in its capacity to serve as a bridge: a bridge that enables us to move freely and easily, without knowing it, between third-dimensional reality and fourth-dimensional reality. A bridge that enables us to practice operating from the love vibration of the latter while existing physically in the former. Such a bridge is necessary because even though deep down we know that fourth-dimensional reality is based on love, peace, oneness, and joy—and we yearn desperately to go there—we are terrified at the thought of letting go of what is all so familiar. This is true even though the current reality is one based on fear, separation, and pain. The doubt is real and deep-seated—what if I jump into the void and find that the other reality doesn't exist after all?

So, while the technology of Radical Forgiveness ostensibly appears to be about helping us forgive ourselves and others, its real purpose is to give us a chance to *practice* being in that other reality while being blissfully ignorant of our actual presence there. It lulls us into thinking that we are simply doing a forgiveness worksheet, or one of the other processes, when in fact we are—without realizing it—actually stepping across that chasm and operating in fourth-dimensional reality. By the use of "smoke and mirrors" and the blessing of ignorance, our ego happily goes along with the process.

Like anything else, the more we practice something, the less fear we have about it. When the time comes for us to make the shift—which I believe is imminent—we will be so accustomed to being in the vibration of the love-based reality (through using Radical Forgiveness) that our fears about making the final leap will have evaporated.

This brings me to a question that people who have just completed one of my workshops frequently ask: "How can I stay in the Radical Forgiveness vibration and not get pulled back into victim consciousness by the world around me?"

The quick answer is simple—keep using the tools. Each and every time we practice Radical Forgiveness, we become more and more anchored in the fourth-dimensional reality and, in turn, it becomes less and less likely that we will choose to return to the third. Eventually, it will become our default way of being, and we will have become fully stabilized at the higher vibratory rate.

But there is a much deeper aspect to this question that we must also address. In order to keep using the tools so that we remain playing in fourth-dimensional reality and raising our vibration, we must stay awake.

Refer to the Victimland Roller Coaster diagram on page 305. Here we see that if we become so upset that we go above the line marking both the loss of spiritual consciousness and our crossing into Victimland, we are in deep trouble. The result is a dramatic lowering of our vibratory rate and the loss of awareness of the newfound reality. We find ourselves back in the world of separation and fear-based reality—back in the grip of the ego. The furthest thing from our mind at this point is doing a worksheet or listening to the *Radical Forgiveness* CD. In short, we are lost.

I now see this phenomenon as not just a setback for the people who lose what they have gained through the Radical Forgiveness experience (as the question about falling back into victim consciousness implies might happen), but as the thing most likely to impede the achievement of the mission to create a world of forgiveness by 2012.

As you know, to create this Awakening, a certain critical mass of people whose consciousness is sufficiently raised to counteract the many whose vibratory rate remains low is required. It is critical, therefore, that all those who have had their vibration raised (even by reading this book), remain awake and engaged in the very process that keeps them traversing that bridge.

Until now, my primary goal in using Radical Forgiveness has been to heal our wounds and release energy blocks in order to improve our lives—not that I have restricted it to working with individuals, for I have found it to be every bit as potent a technology for healing communities. Working in Australia gave me the opportunity to try it in the context of the reconciliation movement that is happening there as white and aboriginal Australians come together to heal their terrible past. I wrote and published a book there called *Reconciliation Through Radical Forgiveness: A Spiritual Technology for Healing Communities*. This book was designed to give everyone in Australia who wanted reconciliation the spiritual technology to bring it about—something they could use in their own homes, schools, and communities. I am doing the same thing now with corporations.

So yes, of course this work will continue, but my colleagues and I at the Institute for Radical Forgiveness are also extending that focus to include helping people not only to maintain the high vibratory rate gained during the Radical Forgiveness experience, but to increase it steadily to as high a level as possible so that there will be no going back.

To this end, we have created a Radical Empowerment program designed to enable people to operate from a higher-than-normal vibratory rate, and, instead of always being the *effect* in a cause-and-effect world, to become the *cause* in their own life. Radical Empowerment is a combination of Radical Forgiveness (to clean up the past and deal effectively with the present), and Radical Manifestation (to create the future). Hence the formula: $RE = RF + RM$. Empowered in this way, people will be able to manifest what they want, easily and quickly.

One of the keys to our spiritual empowerment, and central to our maintaining our connection with the Radical Forgiveness vibration, is the systematic development of that part of our consciousness known as the observer. This is the self-aware part of ourselves that is able to witness or observe the whole community of selves within. From its vantage point outside of, or separate from, ourselves, it will, if trained to do so, notice when we begin to go unconscious. It will then take steps to bring us back—probably by reminding us to do the four-step process in that moment, or to listen to the *Radical Forgiveness* CD. A trained observer will keep us out of Victimland—free and always with choice in our lives.

Another question that inevitably comes up is: "How can I effectively apply the Radical Forgiveness technology to every area of my life?"

The answer to this is also contained in the Radical Empowerment program. Once you have integrated the Radical Forgiveness/Radical Manifestation model into your consciousness and developed your observer to a reasonably high degree, you will naturally begin to utilize Radical Empowerment in every aspect of your life. It will be hard not to.

The third question that arises once people realize the potential of this work to make a difference in the world and see in it for themselves the possibility to do meaningful spiritual work, becomes: "How can I share this with others?"

The answer is that we now have in place a professional certification program through which you can be trained to become (a) a Radical Empowerment Teacher, (b) a Radical Forgiveness coach, or (c) a Radical Manifestation coach and workshop facilitator (see Further Resources).

Another way to respond to that question is by pointing out that Radical Forgiveness is a word-of-mouth phenomenon. Back in 1997, when I first published the book, I received a letter from the owner of one of the biggest independent bookstores in Atlanta. She said that she was noticing that people were coming in and buying a copy of the book and then returning a week or so later to buy six more for their friends. She wrote, "I have seen this phenomenon happen only with two other books—*Celestine*

*Prophecy* and *Conversations with God*, both of which have become bestsellers." I am not suggesting necessarily that you go out and buy six books to give away, but you would be contributing in a big way if you simply told your friends about Radical Forgiveness. There is probably no better way these days than to send out an email message to everyone in your address book who you think might be interested.

So there you have it—Radical Forgiveness is finally out of the closet. It has been, as it were, masquerading as simply a way to heal your life (which, of course, it is), but it is now "outed" as being a powerful technology that will, in addition to helping you heal and eradicate blocks in your life, raise your vibration considerably, awaken you fully, and assist you in becoming an empowered spiritual being, fully able to shift easily between the third and fourth—and even the fifth—dimensions of reality.

It is also a way for each of us, both individually and collectively, to make a significant difference in the world. As our vibratory rate increases, we will find ourselves being called to do more to help others and prepare for the great Awakening.

Thank you for being on this journey with me. There is much to look forward to and be excited about, and I am grateful that you are in my life.

*Namasté*
Colin Tipping

# Notes

1  Joan Borysenko, *Guilt Is the Teacher; Love Is the Lesson* (New York: Warner Books, 1990).

2  Ernst Becker, *The Denial of Death* (New York: Macmillan, 1973).

3  Ken Carey, *The Starseed Transmission* (New York: HarperOne, 1991).

4  For a thorough explanation of how our evolution can be explained by reference to the chakras, see Caroline Myss, *Anatomy of the Spirit* (New York: Three Rivers Press, 1996).

5  A. M. Patent, *You Can Have It All* (New York: Simon & Schuster, 1995).

_____, *Death, Taxes, and Other Illusions* (Tucson: Celebration Publishing, 1989).

6  Richard Bach, *Running from Safety: An Adventure of the Spirit* (Concord, CA: Delta, 1995).

# Further Resources

WE HAVE NUMEROUS books, audio programs, videos, and online courses available to help expand your knowledge about and practical use of the Radical Forgiveness technology. We also offer professional training programs that enable you to share Radical Forgiveness with others. To learn more about our products or to find a Radical Forgiveness coach, and opportunities for workshops and Radical Forgiveness Circle Ceremonies, please visit our website at radicalforgiveness.com.

# About the Author

BORN IN ENGLAND in 1941, Colin was raised during the war and in early post-war Britain by working-class parents. He has an elder brother and a younger sister, both of whom appear in Chapter 1, "Jill's Story." By his own account his parents were good people, loving and hardworking, and he considers himself blessed in having had a stable and enjoyable childhood in spite of the social hardships of the time.

Even as a boy, he seemed to inspire the trust of people who needed to talk about their feelings, as they found in him a person who would listen and not judge. After a four-year stint in the Royal Air Force, he became a high school teacher and a college professor, but even then often found himself being sought after to provide counseling for people. He has three children from his first marriage, which ended in divorce after seven years. A second marriage lasted only four, but he nevertheless remains friends with both ex-wives.

He immigrated to America in 1984 and shortly thereafter became certified as a clinical hypnotherapist. He liked hypnotherapy because, after some years of experience, he concluded it speeded up the therapy by a factor of at least three.

He was not religious then and still feels "free" of any organized religious dogma. His spirituality is essentially practical and down-to-earth, simple, free, and open-ended.

In 1992, he and his wife JoAnn, whom he met in Atlanta and married in 1990, created a series of healing retreats in the north Georgia mountains for people challenged by cancer. In recognizing that lack of forgiveness was a big part of the causation, they set about refining a new form of forgiveness which later was to become what is now recognized as Radical Forgiveness. Unlike traditional forgiveness, which takes many years and is universally seen as very difficult to achieve, this had to be be quick, easy to do, simple, and therapy-free.

In 1997, Colin wrote the first edition of this book and began doing workshops in January 1998. He now has an Institute for Radical Forgiveness in the U.S.A., Australia, Poland, and Germany. He has no plans to retire.

# About Sounds True

SOUNDS TRUE WAS founded in 1985 with a clear vision: to disseminate spiritual wisdom. Located in Boulder, Colorado, Sounds True publishes teaching programs that are designed to educate, uplift, and inspire. We work with many of the leading spiritual teachers, thinkers, healers, and visionary artists of our time.

To receive a free catalog of tools and teachings for personal and spiritual transformation, please visit soundstrue.com, call toll-free 800-333-9185, or write to us at the address below.

SOUNDS TRUE
PO Box 8010
Boulder, CO 80306

# Other Products and Resources Available at radicalforgiveness.com

RADICAL FORGIVENESS IS a technology that provides a wide variety of tools, processes, and experiential programs to help you make forgiveness a part of your everyday life.

Many of the tools on our website are free, and we encourage you to use them as often as you like.

There are also paid *Online Programs* specifically designed to help you forgive your parents, your partners, or yourself.

*The Online Radical Manifestation Program* trains you to be a "conscious creator."

*The Online Radical Money Program* enables you to raise your subconscious "income set point" with the goal of quadrupling your income over a period of two years.

*The "Satori" Radical Forgiveness Game* besides being fun and a great way to introduce Radical Forgiveness to others, is a mini-workshop that never fails to bring enlightenment ("satori") to the participants.

The only thing you have to give up with *The Radical Weight Loss Program* are the stories that caused you to gain weight in the first place.

*The Radical Empowerment Program* puts Radical Forgiveness and Radical Manifestation together to empower you to make a difference in the world and to all aspects of your life. This is a twelve-month, multi-media learning program.

*The Miracles* weekend workshop offers the opportunity of working personally with Colin or a facilitator he has trained in releasing a particular grievance. This is always a life-changing experience.

You will find more books by Colin Tipping at radicalforgiveness.com, as well as CDs, DVDs, and many free downloads.

Certification programs are offered online if you wish to learn how to coach or teach others how to use Radical Forgiveness and Radical Manifestation in the lives of others.

radicalforgiveness.com

# Also from Sounds True and Colin Tipping

A downloadable version of the Radical Forgiveness worksheet can be found at soundstrue.com/radicalforgiveness.

The Power of Radical Forgiveness:
An Experience of Deep Emotional
and Spiritual Healing
Colin Tipping
Spoken-Word Audio / F1309D
6 CDs, 5½ hours, 34-page study guide on CD-ROM
US $69.95 / ISBN: 978-1-59179-678-7
UPC: 600835-130929

Radical Forgiveness
Colin Tipping
Spoken-Word Audio / W1455D
3 CDs, including an E-CD
US $24.95 / ISBN: 978-1-59179-767-8
UPC: 600835-145527

Audio products are available on CD and digital download.